The Canadian Press

CAPS and
SPELLING

15th edition

Fully revised
and updated

The Canadian Press
The Last Word. First.

36 King St. East, Toronto, Ontario M5C 2L9
Telephone: 416-364-0321   Fax: 416-364-9283
E-mail: books@cp.org

Canadian Cataloguing in Publication Data
Main entry under title:

(CP) caps and spelling

15th ed.
ISBN 0-920009-22-0

1. English language - Capitalization. 2. English language -
Orthography and spelling. I. Tasko, Patti. II. Canadian Press.
PE1450.C72 2000   428.1   C00-933000-3

First printing 1965 Revised 1969, 1973, 1976, 1978, 1981, 1985,
1986, 1987, 1988, 1990, 1992, 1996, 1998 and 2000.

Copyright 2000 by The Canadian Press

Design and cover art by
Sean Vokey
The Canadian Press

Printed by
Image Plus Graphics
Toronto, Ontario

Foreword

Caps and Spelling was first published in 1965 to bring together in a single booklet the words, proper names and abbreviations most likely to cause problems for editors at Canadian daily newspapers.

Apparently it filled a much wider need, because it was quickly adopted as a standard reference work by other publications, government departments, colleges and businesses across Canada.

In this revision for 2000, *Caps and Spelling* has once again been updated to reflect the needs of today's writing community. Many of the changes and additions to this edition come at the request of the writers and editors who use the CP Stylebook and this book. Thanks go to those alert and loyal editors, both at CP and in organizations across the country, who help keep this reference up to date.

In particular, in this edition, we have placed a special emphasis on expanding our coverage of Internet terminology. We've provided some general guidelines, plus a host of individual listings: dot-com, home page, chat room, hyperlink, FTP, URL and others.

We have also increased the number of listings of Canadian companies, to help our business and corporate editors. And, as usual, we have updated our entertainment references to keep our pop culture editors happy!

This edition also marks a major change in our policy on the spelling of common-noun elements in proper names. CP now uses the common-noun spelling favoured by the subject – for instance, Lincoln Center (not Centre); U.S. Labor Department (not Labour); Canadian Paediatric Society (not Pediatric).

This doesn't mean, however, that we will blindly follow the wishes of companies and other entities that ignore normal capitalization and spelling practices when creating "distinctive" names. The general principle to keep in mind is this: we are writing words, not reproducing a logo. CP style continues to insist that the first letter of a proper name is capped (Eatons, not eatons); but not all-capped (Gap, not GAP); that normal punctuation rules are followed (Yahoo, not Yahoo!); and that special symbols are not part of our alphabet or punctuation conventions ('N Sync, not *NSYNC). See details in Capitalization, No. 23, and Spelling, No. 3, plus under individual listings.

We set these rules to help the reader because the reader, after all, is a good editor's first priority.

Patti Tasko, Editor

Capitalization

1. The Canadian Press follows a modified down style. This is the basic rule:

   Capitalize all proper names, the names of departments and agencies of national and provincial governments, trade names, names of associations, companies, clubs, religions, languages, races, places, addresses. Otherwise, lowercase is favoured where a reasonable option exists.

2. Common nouns — church, league — are capitalized when part of a proper name: Anglican Church, National Hockey League. They are normally lowercased when standing alone: the church's stand, a league spokesman.

3. The common-noun elements of proper nouns are normally lowercase in plural uses: the United and Anglican churches, the National and American leagues.

4. Formal titles directly preceding a name are capitalized: Prime Minister Jean Chrétien, Archbishop T.D. Somerville. They are lowercased standing alone and in plural uses: the prime minister, the archbishop, premiers Lucien Bouchard and Mike Harris.

5. As a rule of thumb, formal titles are those that are almost an integral part of a person's name — they could be used with the surname alone, if that were CP style: Ald. Cowan, Rabbi Steinberg, Sgt. Duplessis.

6. Job descriptions are lowercased: soprano Maria Stratas, managing editor Anne Davies, Acme Corp. chairman Joseph Schultz.

7. Long or cumbersome titles and job descriptions should be set off with commas: Jean Dubois, energy, mines and resources minister, attended. Or: The energy, mines and resources minister, Jean Dubois, attended. An internationally known Canadian architect, Arthur Erickson, was present.

8. All references to the current Pope, Canada's reigning monarch and the current Governor General are capitalized.

9. Titles of nobility, religion and suchlike that are commonly used instead of the personal name are capitalized: Duke of Kent, Anglican Primate of Canada. But the duke, the primate.

10. The names of national legislative bodies, including some short forms, are capitalized: House of Commons, the House, the Commons; U.S. Senate; Knesset. Provincial legislatures and local councils are lowercased: Quebec national assembly, Toronto city council.

11. National and provincial government departments and agencies are capitalized: Health Canada, Defence Department, Ministry of Natural Resources, U.S. Secret Service. Local government departments and boards are lowercased: parks and property department, Halifax welfare department.

12. Upper courts are capitalized: B.C. Supreme Court, Appeal Court. Lower courts are lowercased: juvenile court, magistrate's court.

13. Canada's military forces are capitalized: Canadian Armed Forces, the Forces. For other forces, army, navy and air force are lowercased when preceded by the name of the country: the Greek air force, the U.S. army. This style is intended for consistency since the proper name is not always a combination of country and force: the Royal Navy, the British navy; the Royal Air Force, the British air force.

14. Historical periods, historic events, holy days and other special times are capitalized: Middle Ages, First World War, Prohibition, Christmas Eve, Lent, Education Week, October Crisis.

15. Specific geographical regions and features are capitalized: Western Canada, Far North, Lake Superior, Niagara Peninsula. But northern, southern, eastern and western in terms derived from regions are lowercased: a western Canadian, a southerner, northern customs.

16. Regions not generally known as specific regions are lowercase: southern Ontario, eastern Alberta, northern Newfoundland.

17. Sacred names and the proper names and nicknames of the devil are capitalized: the Almighty, Redeemer, Holy Spirit, Allah, Mother of God, Vishnu, Beelzebub, Father of Lies. But devil, hell and heaven are lowercased.

Capitalization

18. Names of races, nations and the like are capitalized: Inuit, Asian, Arab, French-Canadian. But white and black are lowercased.

19. The principal words of titles of books, plays, movies, paintings and the like are capitalized: A Dictionary of Usage and Style, Androcles and the Lion, Gone With the Wind, Isle of the Dead. Principal words are nouns, pronouns, adjectives, adverbs, verbs, the first and last word of the title, as well as prepositions and conjunctions of four letters or more. For infinitives, use to Go, to Be. Both words of compound adjectives are capitalized: Well-Meaning.

20. Nicknames and fanciful names are capitalized: Speedy Gonzales, Mack the Knife, Third World, the Big Three.

21. Awards and decorations are capitalized: Order of Canada, OC; Victoria Cross, VC. University degrees are lowercased except when abbreviated: master of arts, a master's, MA; doctor of philosophy, PhD.

22. Proper nouns and adjectives now regarded as common nouns are lowercased: brussels sprouts, french fries, draconian, scotch.

23. For all-capital corporate and promotional names, capitalize only the first letters: Via, Visa. For names consisting of two or more words written solid, follow the organization's capitalization: SkyDome, MuchMusic. Uppercase the first letter of corporate and promotional names even if the organization's style is lowercase: Adidas, Citytv. For names of people or performing groups, follow their preference, as long as it doesn't excessively hamper readability.

For a fuller treatment of capitalization,
see the CP Stylebook, chapter Capitalization.

Spelling

1. The Canadian Oxford Dictionary is the authority for Canadian Press spelling with specific exceptions noted in the CP Stylebook and this guide. Where optional forms are given — gobbledegook, gobbledygook — the first listed is CP style.

2. When the spelling of the common-noun element of a proper name differs from CP style – U.S. Labor Department, Center Harbor, N.H., Lincoln Center, Canadian Paediatric Society – use the spelling favoured by the subject.

3. CP ignores symbols in corporate or other names or translates them into accepted punctuation if necessary: 'N Sync, not *NSYNC. Check individual listings.

4. CP style is -our, not -or, for labour, honour and other such words of more than one syllable in which the "u" is not pronounced:

arbour	endeavour	rancour
ardour	favour	rigour
armour	fervour	rumour
behaviour	flavour	saviour
candour	glamour	savour
clamour	harbour	splendour
clangour	honour	tumour
colour	humour	valour
demeanour	labour	vapour
discolour	neighbour	vigour
dishonour	odour	
enamour	parlour	

5. In some forms of these words, however, the "u" is dropped, especially when an -ous ending is added: laborious, rancorous, odorous, honorary.

6. For words in common use, CP style is simple "e" rather than the diphthongs "ae" and "oe." Thus CP style is archeologist, ecumenical, encyclopedia, esthetic, fetus, gynecologist, hemorrhage, medieval, paleontologist, pedagogy and pediatrician.

Spelling

7. Generally, proper names retain the diphthong: Caesar, Oedipus, Phoebe. Also hors d'oeuvre, manoeuvre and subpoena. The "ae" in aerial, aerate and such is considered normal spelling.

8. The umlaut — ä, ö and ü — in German names is indicated by the letter "e" after the letter affected. Thus: Goering for Göring.

9. The -ov and -ev endings for Russian names are used instead of -off and -eff. Exceptions include such familiar names as Rachmaninoff, Smirnoff and Ignatieff, where the spelling is established.

10. CP style for First Nations names is to follow the preference of the band. For a current list of bands and their preferred spellings, check the Publications and Research page (community profiles) on the Web site of the Department of Indian and Northern Affairs (www.inac.gc.ca).

Abbreviations

1. All-capital abbreviations are written without periods (YMCA, AFL-CIO, CN, MP, DSO, RIP, UN) unless the abbreviation is geographical (U.S., B.C., P.E.I., T.O.) refers to a person (J.R. Ewing, J.R.) or is a single letter (N. for north but NNW).

2. Most lowercase and mixed abbreviations take periods: f.o.b., Jr., Ont., No., B.Comm.

3. Mixed abbreviations that begin and end with a capital letter do not take periods: PhD, PoW, U of T, MiG.

4. Acronyms — abbreviations pronounced as words — formed from only the first letter of each principal word are all capitals: AIDS (acquired immune deficiency syndrome), NATO (North Atlantic Treaty Organization), NOW (National Organization for Women).

5. Acronyms formed from initial and other letters are upper and lowercase: Dofasco (Dominion Foundries and Steel Corp.), Nabisco (National Biscuit Co.), Norad (North American Aerospace Defence Command).

6. Acronyms that have become common words are not capitalized: laser (light amplification by stimulated emission of radiation), radar (radio detection and ranging).

7. Metric symbols are not abbreviations and do not take periods: m, l, kW.

8. Plurals are MPs and PoWs; possessives MPs' and MP's.

9. Most abbreviations are written without spaces: U.K., W.Va., P.Eng. But those written without periods are spaced: R and D, U of T.

See also the CP Stylebook, chapter
Abbreviations and acronyms.

Place Names

1.   National Geographic Society spellings are CP style for place names outside Canada with exceptions listed in the CP Stylebook and this guide.

2.   The style authority for Canadian place names is the Canadian Oxford Dictionary, with some exceptions listed in this guide. If the place name is not in Oxford, consult the Secretariat of the Canadian Permanent Committee on Geographical Names (http://.geonames.nrcan.gc.ca/). For French place names, see next page.

French Capitalization

1. For the French names of organizations and the titles of books, songs, plays, movies, paintings and the like, CP prefers the English form for the sake of readability: Quebec Liquor Corp., not Société des alcools du Québec; Remembrance of Things Past, not A la recherche du temps perdu.

2. In general, when the French name or title is used (in a quotation, for example) it should be followed by a translation in parentheses: Office de la langue française (French Language Board), Le Malade imaginaire (The Imaginary Invalid).

3. If a work, organization or the like is commonly known by its French name, it need not be followed by a translation: La Bohème, Notre Dame, Le Droit.

4. The names of some organizations cannot really be translated (Conseil du patronat, the largest employer group in Quebec), or have become familiar in their French version (the Ecole polytechnique, the engineering school), or have no official English version (the Centrale de l'enseignement du Québec, the teachers federation). Such titles should be treated as exceptions, and additions to the list should be made reluctantly.

5. CP uses hyphens in multi-word French place names in Quebec and abroad: Trois-Rivières, Ste-Anne-de-Beaupré, Stanstead-Est, Ver-sur-Mer. Hyphens are omitted from purely English place names: Stanstead Plain, and if the first word is not a place name but a natural feature: Lac Barrière, Baie des Chaleurs.

6. For the names of saints (except in place names) use St. (not Ste.) for female as well as male: St. Dorothee.

7. CP's French dictionaries are Le Petit Robert and Le Petit Larousse.

French Names

1. For the names of organizations, the first word is capitalized unless it is an article; other words except proper nouns are lowercase: (le) Service de perception, Emballages St-Laurent ltée.

2. For the titles of books, songs and the like, the first word is capitalized — the second too when the first is an article — and proper nouns: De la terre à la lune, Sur le pont d'Avignon, Les Liaisons dangereuses.

3. For the names of newspapers, the definite article, the first noun and proper nouns are capitalized: Le Journal de Montréal, Le Courrier du peuple.

A

A, An–Use "a" before consonant sounds: a historic
building, a university, a one-way ticket, a euphemism,
a 1914 novel. Use "an" before vowel sounds: an apple,
an honest man, an S-bend, an 1814 novel.

A&E (specialty TV channel)

A&P (acceptable in all references for
Great Atlantic and Pacific Tea Co.)

A&W

ABC (acceptable in all references for American
Broadcasting Cos. — note plural)

abattoir

abhor, abhorrence, abhorrent

Abidjan

Abitibi-Consolidated Inc.

able seaman (*no abbvn.*)

A-bomb

abominable snowman (yeti)

aboriginal (*adj., n. when referring to individual*); in
Australia: Aboriginal or Aborigine

Aboriginal Peoples (all of Canada's Indians, Inuit and
Métis)

abscess

abysmal (*not* -ss-)

abyss

Acadie nouvelle, L' (newspaper in Caraquet, N.B.)

accessible *(not* -able)

accommodate (-mm-), accommodation

acetaminophen

acetylene

acetylsalicylic acid (ASA)

Achilles heel, tendon

acknowledgment

acquit, acquitted, acquittal

Act–Capitalize titles of parliamentary acts but
not subsequent references when the full
name is not used. And references to acts
and bills before royal assent are lowercase.
–Food and Drugs Act
–National Housing Act (NHA, *but avoid*)

11

–the housing act says ...

–a proposed housing act

Act 3, Scene 2; the third act, second scene

acting, acting mayor James Borden

ACTRA (Alliance of Canadian Cinema, Television and Radio Artists)

AD–Acceptable in all references for anno Domini (in the year of the Lord). The abbreviation goes before the figure for the year: AD 410. It may also be used to refer to a century: the first century AD.

adaptability

addendum, addenda

Addresses–Capitalize Street, Road, etc., used with names; *but* King and Victoria streets. Abbreviate in addresses when the number is used; *but* 10 Downing Street, 24 Sussex Drive (official residences).

–36 King St. E., Toronto M5C 2L9

–the Portage Avenue bus

–Wellington Crescent

–Cres., Blvd., Rd., Sq.

Adidas (*not* adidas)

adieu, adieus

adjuster (*not* -or)

administration, U.S. administration

Admiral John Smith (*no abbvn.*)

–the admiral said ...

admiralty

–the admiralty reported ...

–first lord of the admiralty

–the first lord's statement

–Admiralty Court

admissible (*not* -able), admissibility

ad nauseam (*not* -eum)

Adonai

Adventist, Seventh-day

adverse (unfavourable), averse (reluctant)

advertise (*not* -ize)

adviser (*not* -or)
aerial
aerodynamics
Aeroflot airline
Aeronautics Act
aesthetic — *Use* esthetic
AF and AM (for Ancient Free and Accepted
  Masons, *but avoid*)
  –a Freemason, a Mason
affect (*v.* — have effect on)
affidavit
affront (deliberate insult), effrontery
  (shameless insolence)
Afghan
aficionado (*one f*), aficionados
AFL-CIO (acceptable in all references for
  American Federation of Labor-Congress
  of Industrial Organizations)
African-American
Afrikaans (language)
Afrikaner (person)
Aga Khan, the
Agence France-Presse (AFP)
agenda, agendas
agent provocateur, agents provocateurs
aggression, aggressive
aging (*not* ageing)
agreement
  –a Canada-U.S. agreement on power
  –General Agreement on Tariffs and
  Trade (GATT)
aide-de-camp, aides-de-camp
AIDS (for acquired immune deficiency
  syndrome)
air bag (*two words*)
airbase (*one word*)
Airbus
Air Canada (*no abbvn.*)
Air Commodore John Smith (*no abbvn.*)

A

—the air commodore said ...

Aircraft Names—Use a hyphen between symbols for the make
or type and the model number.

—DC-8L, B-57, A-320, MiG-25, CF-18

—Yak-42, AN-154, IL-62, TU-144

—*but* Dash 8 (*no hyphen*)

aircrew (*one word*)

airdrop (*one word*)

Air Force—Capitalize air force in references
to the pre-unification Royal Canadian Air
Force. For other forces, lowercase air
force when preceded by the name of the
country.

—British air force

—Royal Air Force

—U.S. or American air force

—U.S. 8th Air Force

—the air force planes

—Bomber Command

—Coastal Command

—Fleet Air Arm

—126 Squadron

—the squadron headquarters are ...

Air India (*no hyphen*)

airlift (*n. and v.*)

airmail (*n. and v.*)

airman (*no abbvn.*)

Air Marshal Lois Jones (*no abbvn.*)

—the air marshal said ...

Air Miles (loyalty program)

Airport—Lowercase unless the official name
is used.

—Pearson International Airport

—Toronto international airport

—Vancouver International Airport

—the Vancouver airport

air strike

Air Vice-Marshal John Candy (*no abbvn.*)

—the air vice-marshal

Aklavik, N.W.T.
Alabama (Ala.)
Alaska (*no abbvn.*)
Alberta Heritage Savings Trust Fund (*no abbvn.*)
albino, albinos
Alcan Aluminium Ltd.
Alcoholics Anonymous (AA)
    –Al-Anon (for relatives of alcoholics)
    –Alateen (for children of alcoholics)
alderman (Ald.)
    –Ald. John Doe
    –aldermen Bill Jones and John Wong
alga, algae
Algonquian (aboriginal language family)
Algonquin (Ojibwa dialect)
Allah
Allahu akbar! (God is great)
all-America (team), all-American (individual)
Allan Cup (hockey)
Alliance Atlantis Communications Inc.
Alliance of Canadian Cinema, Television
    and Radio Artists (ACTRA)
Alliance of Manufacturers & Exporters Canada (formerly
    Canadian Manufacturers' Association and Canadian
    Exporters' Association)
Allied forces, the Allies (in world wars)
allophone (*but avoid*)
allot, allotted, allotting
all ready (set to go), already (beforehand)
all right (*two words; not* alright)
All Saints' Day (Nov. 1)
all-star
    –an all-star team, game
    –CP's all-star selections
    –National League All-Stars (team)
allusion (indirect reference), illusion (false
    impression)
Almighty, the
Alouette 1, 2 (satellites)

Alps, *but* alpine skiing
already (beforehand)
alternate (one after the other), alternative
    (one or the other)
aluminium (chemical element)
    –Alcan Aluminium Ltd.
    –British Aluminium Ltd.
aluminum (metal)
    –Aluminum Co. of Canada Ltd.
    –Aluminum Co. of America, Alcoa
    (in U.S.)
    –*but* Alcan Aluminium Ltd.
alumna (*fem.*), alumnae
alumnus (*masc.*), alumni
Alzheimer's disease (*but* Alzheimer
    Society of Canada)
a.m., p.m. (*lowercase*)
    –2 p.m., 2:30 a.m. EST, EDT
amalgam, amalgamate
a mari usque ad mare
ambience
amendment, Fifth Amendment (U.S.)
American Federation of Labor-Congress of
    Industrial Organizations (AFL-CIO)
American Indian Movement (AIM)
American Telephone and Telegraph Co.
    (AT&T, *but* ITT)
America's Cup (yachting)
amiable (of people), amicable (of things)
amok (*not* amuck)
Ampersand–Use when part of a corporate name;
    otherwise avoid.
    –AT&T Canada *but* Ian and Sylvia
Amtrak (*not* Amtrack)
Anacin (trademark for a painkiller)
analogous
analogue, analogue computer, data
analyse (*not* -ze), analysing
analysis, analyses

anemia, anemic

anesthesia, anesthetic, anesthetist

aneurysm

Anglican Church of Canada

    –Anglican communion

    –Anglican Church Women

    –High Church, Low Church

Anglo, Anglo-Quebecer, Anglos

anglophone (*lowercase*)

Anik E-1, E-2 (satellites)

Animals–Capitalize breed names derived
    from proper names except where usage
    has established the lowercase.

    –Holstein-Friesian *but* shorthorn

    –Clydesdale *but* palomino

    –Newfoundland dog *but* dachshund

    –Siamese cat *but* angora

anoint

anomaly, anomalies

anorexia nervosa, anorexic

ante (prefix), antechamber, antedate,
    antenatal, anteroom

antenna, antennae (*pl.* for feelers of insect,
    etc.), antennas (*pl.* for aerials)

anti- (*prefix*), anti-aircraft, anti-Communist,
    antihistamine, anti-intellectual
    anti-Semitic, antitrust, antiwar

antivenene (*not* anti-venom)

anybody

anyhow

anymore (any longer)

any more (*as in* "I don't want any more candy")

anyone

anything

any time (*two words*)

anyway

AOL Canada Inc. (*not* America Online Canada)

apartheid

Apartment–Capitalize when used specifically,

as when followed by a number; abbreviate when used in numbered addresses.
–the Rockingham Apartments
–in Apt. 207
–Apt. 207, Midtown Terrace
APEC (Asia-Pacific Economic Cooperation)
apostle, Twelve Apostles
–the Apostle Paul
–Paul the Apostle
appal, appalled, appalling
Appaloosa
apparatus, apparatuses
appeal, appealed, appealing, appealingly
Appeal Court
appellant
appellate division (of Supreme Court)
appendix, appendixes
Apples–Capitalize varieties.
–McIntosh Red, Delicious
–Yellow Transparent
April (*no abbvn.*)
April Fool's Day (April 1)
Aqaba, Gulf of
Aqua-Lung (trademark for an underwater
breathing device)
aquarium, aquariums
arabic numerals
Arafat, Yasser (PLO leader)
Aransas (*not* Arkansas) refuge
arbour
arc, arcing, arced
Arcand, Denys (movies)
Archbishop–Capitalize before a name and
when the full title is used.
–Archbishop John Smith
–Archbishop of York
–the archbishop said ...
archeological, archeologist, archeology
Arctic, Arctic Circle, Arctic Ocean (geographic

features); arctic char, arctic cold,
arctic fox, arctic plant, arctic winds
(characteristic of, native to the Arctic)

ardour

Argentine (*not* Argentinian)

argyle socks, sweater

Argyll and Sutherland Highlanders of Canada

Arizona (Ariz.)

Arkansas (Ark.) *but* Aransas refuge (for
wildlife)

Armed Forces, the Forces (capped for Canada
only)

armful, armfuls

armour

Army–Capitalize Canadian Army when referring to
pre-unification force. For other forces, lowercase army
when preceded by the name of the country.
–Canadian Army until 1968
–British army
–British 21st Army
–a convoy of army vehicles
–1st Canadian Division
–3rd Infantry Brigade
–Royal 22nd Regiment
–1st Battalion, Royal 22nd
–B Company

Art Deco

arteriosclerosis

Arthabaska, Que. (Athabasca, Alta.)

arthroscopy

article
–a paragraph of Article 4
–Art. 4, Sec. 1, reads:

artifact

Arviat, Nunavut (formerly Eskimo Point)

Aryan Nations (white supremacist group)

ascend, ascendance, ascendant, ascension,
ascent
–Ascension Day

A

Ashrawi, Hanan (Palestinian)
Ash Wednesday
asinine
Aspirin (trademark in Canada)
Assad, Hafez (Syria)
assassin, assassination
assembly
> –National Assembly (national legislative body)
> –Quebec national assembly (provincial body)
> –legislative assembly

assistant (*lowercase*), assistant attorney general Karen Williams
assizes, spring assizes
Associated Press, The (for AP)
> –and The Associated Press said ...
> –the Associated Press story said ...

Association of South East Asian Nations (ASEAN)
Associations–Capitalize names, but follow French style for French names.
> –Société pour vaincre la pollution
> –Association of the Scientific, Engineering and Technological Community of Canada (Scitec)
> –Canadian Bankers Association
> –the association meeting

asthma
Astronomy–Capitalize the proper names of planets, stars, constellations; capitalize only the proper-noun element of the name of comets, etc.; lowercase sun and moon. In general, lowercase earth, but capitalize it when referred to as an astronomical body.
> –Saturn, North Star, Orion
> –Halley's comet, Crab nebula
> –down to earth

—heaven on earth
—The planets closest to the sun are Mercury, Venus and Earth.
—The astronauts turned back to Earth.

Astroturf (trademark for artificial grass or turf)

AT&T (*no spaces*), for American Telephone and Telegraph Co.

Athabasca, Alta. (Arthabaska, Que.)

Athapaskan (aboriginal languages)

atherosclerosis (a form of arteriosclerosis with fatty degeneration)

Athlete of the Year

athlete's foot

Atikamekw (First Nations in Quebec)

Atlantic provinces (N.B., Nfld., N.S., P.E.I.)

Atomic Energy of Canada Ltd. (AECL, *but avoid*)

attorney, Crown
—Crown attorney Ellen Tomcik
—power of attorney (*no hyphens*)

attorney general, attorneys general
—Attorney General John Devon

Audit Bureau of Circulations (ABC)

auditor general, auditors general

auger (tool for boring holes)

augur (bode)

Augustyn, Frank (ballet)

aurora borealis (northern lights); aurora australis (southern equivalent)
—Aurora (patrol aircraft)

authority
—St. Lawrence Seaway Authority

authorize

autogyro

automaker, autoworker (*but* Canadian Auto Workers union)

automaton, automatons

auto pact (signed January 1965)

A

auxiliary, auxiliaries

Avenue–Capitalize when used with names;
abbreviate in numbered street addresses.
–along Portage Avenue
–the Portage Avenue bus
–506 Curry Ave., Windsor, Ont. N9B 2B9

averse (reluctant), adverse (unfavourable)

avocado, avocados

Avro Arrow (the CF-105 interceptor aircraft
built by A.V. Roe Canada Ltd. in the
1950s)

AWACS (for airborne warning and control
system)

Awards–Capitalize specific awards.
–National Newspaper Awards (NNA)
–the awards were presented ...
–Governor General's Awards
–Governor General's Award for poetry
–Nobel Peace Prize
–Nobel Prize in chemistry
–Nobel Prize winner
–Pulitzer Prize
–Pulitzer Prize-winning author
–Academy Awards

AWL (*not* AWOL — absent without leave; *but
avoid*)

axe (*not* ax), axing

Axel (figure-skating jump)

axis, axes
–Axis, the (Second World War alliance of
Germany, Italy and Japan)

Aykroyd, Dan (comic)

Azerbaijan

AZT (AIDS drug azidothymidine; now called
zidovudine)

Baathist party (Iraq)
baby boom, baby boom generation
babysit, babysitter
baccalaureate
Bachand, Andre (politician)
Bachand, Claude (politician)
bachelor
>   –bachelor of arts (BA), a bachelor's
>   degree
>   –bachelor of laws (LLB, *but avoid*)
>   –bachelor of science (B.Sc.)
bacillus, bacilli
backbench members, backbenchers
backbone, backlog, backstop (*n.* and *v.*)
back burner
backstage
bacterium, bacteria
Baggies (trademark for plastic bags)
Baghdad Pact
Baha'i (*n.* and *adj.*)
>   –two Baha'is
>   –the Baha'i faith
Bahamas, the
Bahamian (*not* Bahaman)
Bahrain
bail (water or bond)
bail out (of plane)
baked alaska
balaclava
bale (hay)
balk
balkanize
ball, ball club, ball game, ball park, ball player
balloon, ballooning, balloonist
ballot, balloting
ballpoint
ballroom, Crystal Ballroom
baloney (slang — nonsense; also
>   informal — bologna sausage)

band, the God's River band
Band-Aid (trademark for an adhesive
      bandage)
banister (*not* -nn-)
banjo, banjos
Banks–Short forms may be used on first
      reference when their use is
      widespread.
      –Bank of Canada
      –the bank's lending policy
      –Bank of Nova Scotia, Scotiabank
      –CIBC, Canadian Imperial
      Bank of Commerce
      –Hongkong Bank of Canada
      –Royal Bank of Canada, the Royal
      –Toronto Dominion Bank, TD Bank
      –World Bank
baptize (*not* -s-)
bar
      –Canadian Bar Association (CBA, *but*
      avoid)
      –Bar of the Province of Quebec
      (organization)
      –*but* Quebec bar, Montreal bar, called
      to the bar
barbecue (*not* -que), barbecuing
Bardot, Brigitte
barefoot (*no hyphen*)
bar mitzvah (for boy marking 13th birthday),
      bat mitzvah (for girl)
Barnard, Dr. Christiaan
Barren Lands, the Barrens
Barrick Gold Inc.
Baryshnikov, Mikhail (ballet)
Baseball–at bat (*but* five at-bats), backstop,
      ball club, ball park, ball player, baseline, bullpen, cen-
      tre field, centre-fielder,
      centre-field fence, change-up,
      doubleheader, double-play, fastball, first

baseman, home plate, home run,
left-fielder, left-hander, line up (*v.*),
lineup (*n.*), major league (*n.*),
major-league (*adj.*), a major-leaguer (*n.*),
put out (*v.*), putout (*n.*), pinch hit
(*n.* and *v.*), pinch-hitter (*n.*), play off (*v.*),
playoff (*n., adj.*), RBI(s), right-fielder,
right-hander, shortstop, shut out (*v.*),
shutout (*n., adj.*), split-finger fastball,
triple-play, twi-night doubleheader

Basel, Switzerland

BASIC (for beginner's all-purpose symbolic
instruction code)

basis, bases

Basketball–backboard, backcourt, baseline,
field goal, foul line, foul shot, free throw,
free-throw line, frontcourt, full-court
press, goaltending, half-court pass,
halftime, in-bounds pass, jump ball,
jump shot, layup, man-to-man (*adj.*),
midcourt, play off (*v.*), playoff (*n., adj.*),
three-point play, three-pointer

basset (dog)

battalion, 3rd Battalion

Battle Harbour, Nfld.

Battles–Capitalize specific ones.
    –Battle of the Plains of Abraham
    –Battle of Britain

bay, Hudson Bay, Bay of Quinte
    –Hudson's Bay Co., the Bay

bazaar

BB (shot)

BBS (computer bulletin board system; spell out in
first reference)

BC–Acceptable in all references for before
Christ. It follows the year or the century:
55 BC, the second century BC.

BCE Emergis Inc.

BCE Inc. (formerly Bell Canada Enterprises)

B

beau, beaus
bedeck (adorn), bedecked
beef Stroganoff
Beethoven, Ludwig van (*not* von)
  (1770-1827)
behaviour
behoove (*not* behove)
Beijing (formerly Peking)
Belarus (formerly Byelorussia)
Belize (formerly British Honduras)
Bell Canada
Bellehumeur, Michel (politician)
belligerent
bellwether
Belmont Stakes
beluga (whale)
Ben (son of)–Capitalize in Arabic names.
benediction
benefit, benefited, benefiting
Benin (Dahomey until 1975)
Benzedrine (trademark)
Bergeron, Stephane (politician)
Berkeley, Calif.
Berlin Wall
Bermudian (*not* Bermudan)
Bern, Switzerland
Bernhard, Prince (Netherlands)
berserk
Berton, Pierre
Beverly Hills, Calif.
besieged (*not* beseiged)
best-seller, best-selling author
bettor (one who wagers)
bias, biased
Bible, Bible Belt
        –*but* the fisherman's bible
biblical
Bic (trademark for pen)
bicultural, bilingual (*no hyphen*)

B

Bid.com International Inc.

Biennial, bimonthly, biweekly–These terms
are ambiguous and can mean two
different things. *Prefer* every two
years, twice a month, twice a week, etc.

Big Three, Big Ten

big-time (*adj.*)

bill

–Bill 101

–a proposed bill of rights

billet, billeted, billeting

Binghamton, N.Y.

Biochem Pharma Inc.

biracial (*no hyphen*)

birdie (one stroke under par)

Birks Jewellers (store)

–Henry Birks and Sons Ltd.

Birney, Earle (poet, 1904-1995)

birth, birthday, birthmark, birthrate,
birthright

Bishkek, Kyrgyzstan (formerly Frunze,
Kirghizia)

Bishop–Capitalize before a name and when
the full title is used.

–Bishop Edward Tremaine

–Bishop of London

–the bishop's letter

Bismarck (*not* -rk)

black (*prefer to* Negro)

blackfly, blackflies

Blackhawks, Chicago

Black Muslim (member of Black Muslims
organization; official name: the Nation of Islam)

black out (*v.*), blackout (*n.* and *adj.*)

Black Panther (member of Black Panthers
organization)

Blaikie, Bill (politician)

bleached-kraft pulp

blindsided

27

B

bloc (of parties, countries; voted as a bloc)
   –Bloc Québécois
   –former East Bloc
block (of shares, seats; also mental block)
blond (*n.* and *adj.* for all uses; do not use
   blonde)
Blondin-Andrew, Ethel (politician)
Bloody Mary (nickname for Mary I), bloody
   mary (cocktail)
blue, Double Blue (Argonauts)
blue-line (hockey)
Bluenose II (ship)
B-movie
B'nai Brith (Sons of the Covenant)
board
   –Board of Trade
   –Canadian Wheat Board
   –Ontario Energy Board
   –Treasury Board
   –public school board
   –Saskatoon board of education
boat, lifeboat, motorboat, powerboat, sailboat
bobsled, bobsledding, but Canadian Bobsleigh
   and Luge Association
bodycheck
bodyguard (*no hyphen*)
bogey, bogeys, bogeyed (for one over par)
bohemian (unconventional);
   Bohemian (of Czech region)
boldface (type)
Bomarc-A, Bomarc-B
bombardier (*no abbvn.*)
Bombardier Inc.
bombshell (*one word*)
bona fide (*adj.* — genuine; *adv.* — genuinely),
   bona fides (*n.* — proof of status)
bonspiel
bonus, bonuses
bookkeeper, bookkeeping

Book of Common Prayer

Book of Revelation (*not* Revelations)

Bophuthatswana (former homeland state in South
    Africa)

Borotsik, Rick (politician)

borscht, Borscht Belt

Bosnia-Herzegovina, Bosnia

botanical, botanist, botany

Bouctouche, N.B.

Boulevard–Capitalize when used with names;
    abbreviate in numbered street addresses.
    –on Decarie Boulevard
    –123 Decarie Blvd.

bound (*suffix*), eastbound, northbound,
    stormbound

bourbon (whisky)

Bourgeoys, St. Marguerite (Canada's first
    woman saint, 1620-1700)

Boutros-Ghali, Boutros (UN)

bowl, Rose Bowl, Super Bowl

bowling
    –fivepin, tenpin

boxcar

box office

boyfriend, girlfriend

Boxing–Most weight classes are one word:
    flyweight, bantamweight, heavyweight.
    –knockout

boy scout–*See scout*

braggadocio

braille

Brantford Expositor

Brascan Corp.

Brasilia (capital of Brazil)

Bravo (*not* Bravo!) specialty channel

breach (*n.* — breaking or neglect; *v.* — break
    through)

break (*n.*), breakaway, breakdown, breakfast,
    break-in, breakneck, breakout, breakup,

breakthrough, breakwater

break (*v.*), break away, break down, break
even, break in, break off, break out,
break up

breastfeed

breathalyser

Brébeuf, St. Jean de (1593-1649)

breech (back part of gun barrel), breeches
(short trousers), breeches-buoy

Breitkreuz, Cliff (politician)

Breitkreuz, Garry (politician)

Bren gun

Bre-X Minerals Ltd.

Brezhnev, Leonid (1906-1982)

bridge, Lions Gate Bridge, Sydney Harbour
Bridge

Brier (curling tournament)

brigadier (Brig. Arthur Smith)

brigadier-general (Brig.-Gen. Arthur Smith)

Brillo (trademark for soap pads)

Brink's Canada Ltd.
–*but* a Brinks truck, Brinks guard (*no apostrophe*)

Britain–The one island: England, Scotland,
Wales. (*But* British also covers Northern
Ireland.)

Britannia

British Airways (*no abbvn.*)

British Commonwealth (*prefer* the Commonwealth)

British North America Act (BNA Act)

British thermal unit(s), BTU(s)

Briton (*not* Britisher)

broach (open; begin to talk about)

Brockville Recorder and Times

broccoli

Broken Hill Proprietary Co.
-BHP (common reference)

Bromo Seltzer (trademark for bicarbonate of soda)

brooch (ornament)

Bros. for company names *but* Brothers with
>entertainment groups: the Good Brothers

brouhaha

brussels sprouts

Brzezinski, Zbigniew

Buckingham Palace

Buddha, Buddhism, Buddhist

budget, budgetary, budgeted, budgeting

buffalo, buffaloes

Building–Capitalize important buildings.
>–Parliament Buildings
>–Empire State Building
>–Aetna Life building

build up (*v.*), buildup (*n., adj.*), built-up (*adj*)

Bujold, Geneviève (films)

bulimia

Bullock, Sandra (actress)

bull's-eye

bumf (papers, documents)

bungee jumping

Bunyan, Paul

buoy, buoyant, buoyancy

bureau, bureaus

Burkina Faso (formerly Upper Volta)

Burk's Falls, Ont.

Burton, Richard (1925-1984)

bus (vehicle), buses, busing

businessman, businesswoman

buss (kiss), busses

Buthelezi, Mangosuthu (Zulu leader)

buttonhole (*no hyphen*)

byelection (*no hyphen*)

bylaw (*no hyphen*)

byline (*no hyphen*)

bypass (*no hyphen*)

byplay (*no hyphen*)

byproduct (*no hyphen*)

byte (unit of computer memory)

C

cabinet, cabinet council
cable TV (*no hyphen*)
cacophony
cactus, cacti
cadet
     –officer cadet (*no abbvn.*)
     –Officer Cadet Garth Atkins
Cadillac
CAE Inc.
Caesar, Julius (c. 102-44 BC)
caesarean birth, section (*lowercase*)
caesar salad
Caesars Palace (Las Vegas — *no apostrophe*)
café
caffeine
Cage, Nicolas (actor)
caisse populaire (credit union), caisses
     populaires
Calder Memorial Trophy (NHL's top rookie)
calibre, a .45-calibre pistol
California (Calif.)
Callaghan, Morley (novelist, 1903-1990)
Callbeck, Catherine (senator)
callisthenics
Call-Net Enterprises Inc.
callous (*adj.* — unfeeling), callus
     (*n.* — thickened skin)
calorie
camaraderie
Cambodia (Kampuchea 1975-90)
Canada
     –Central Canada (Ontario and Quebec)
     –Eastern Canada (the Atlantic
     provinces, Quebec and Ontario)
     –Lower Canada (present-day Quebec)
     –Upper Canada (present-day Ontario)
     –Western Canada (Manitoba,
     Saskatchewan, Alberta and
     British Columbia)

C

Canada AM (CTV show)

Canada Council

Canada Cup (hockey)

Canada Customs, customs
  –go through customs, a customs officer

Canada Customs and Revenue Agency (formerly
  Revenue Canada)

Canada Day (July 1)

Canada Labour Relations Board (CLRB, *but
  avoid*)

Canada Life Financial Corp.

Canada Medal (*no abbvn.*)

Canada Mortgage and Housing Corp.
  (CMHC)

Canada News Wire (CNW in second reference)

Canada Pension Plan (CPP, *but avoid*)

Canada Savings Bond (CSB)

Canada's Cup (yachting)

Canada West Foundation

Canada-wide (*adj.*)

Canadian Air Line Pilots Association
  (CALPA)

Canadian Airlines International Ltd.,
  Canadian Airlines (or Canadian if
  meaning clear)

Canadian Alliance (OK in first reference for
  Canadian Reform Conservative Alliance)

Canadian Armed Forces, the Armed Forces,
  the Forces (*capped for Canadian only*)

Canadian Association of Broadcasters (CAB)

Canadian Bankers Association

Canadian Blood Services

Canadian Coast Guard
  –the coast guard ship
  –coastguardman (*one word*)

Canadian Community Newspapers Association

Canadian Conference of Catholic Bishops
  (*not* Council)

Canadian Forces

C

–Canadian Forces Headquarters
(CFHQ, *but avoid*)
–a Canadian Forces base
–Canadian Forces Base Trenton
–CFB Trenton (*second reference or placeline*)
Canadian government
Canadian Hockey Association
Canadian Imperial Bank of Commerce
(CIBC permitted in first reference)
Canadian Institutes of Health Research (formerly
Medical Research Council of Canada)
Canadian National, or CN
–Canadian National Railway Co. (formal
name)
–CN Tower
Canadian National Institute for the Blind
(CNIB)
Canadian Newspaper Association (CNA, *but avoid*)
Canadian Nuclear Safety Commission (formerly
Atomic Energy Control Board)
Canadian Open golf title, tournament
Canadian Opera Company (*not* Co.)
Canadian Pacific Ltd.
–Canadian Pacific Railway, or CPR on
second reference (formerly CP Rail)
–Canadian Pacific Hotels & Resorts
–CP Ships
Canadian Paediatric Society
Canadian Press, The (CP)
–The Canadian Press says ...
–*but* the Canadian Press reporter
Canadian Professional Golfers' Association
(CPGA)
Canadian Radio-television and Telecommuni-
cations Commission (CRTC)
Canadian Security Intelligence Service (CSIS)
Canadian Shield
Canadian Transport Commission (*no abbvn.*)
Canadian Wheat Board (*no abbvn.*)

C

Canadian Wildlife Service (*no abbvn.*)

canal, Panama Canal, Suez Canal, Welland Canal
—Panama Canal Zone, Love Canal
(district)

cancel, cancelled, cancelling

Cancer, Tropic of

CanCom, Canadian Satellite
Communications Inc.

candidacy

candour

Candu (for Canadian deuterium uranium
reactor)

Canfor Corp.

canister

CanLit (informal for Canadian literature)

canoeist

cantaloupe

canto, cantos

Canuck

Canuel, Rene (politician)

canvas, canvases (cloth, painting)

canvass (*v.* — examine; seek votes, orders;
n. — process of canvassing)

Canwest Global Communications Corp.

canyon, Grand Canyon

Cap-aux-Meules, Que.

Cape Breton (*never in placeline*)

Cape Town (*two words*)

Capitol (building at Washington)
but state capitol (*lowercase*)

cappuccino, cappuccinos

captain, Capt. (*but* team captain Joan Verona)

carat (gems), karat (gold), caret (printing)

carburetor

cardinal (*no abbvn.*)
—John Cardinal Smith
—the cardinal (or Smith) said ...

CARE (for Co-operative for American Relief
Everywhere Inc.)

caregiver

cargo, cargoes

Caribbean Community (federation)

Caribbean Free Trade Area (Carifta, *but avoid*)

Cariboo Mountains (B.C.)

Caribou Mountains (Alta.)

caribou (deer), Caribou (Inuit, plane)

carillon, carillonneur

carjack, carjacking (*v.* and *n.*)

Carleton, N.S. and Que.

–Carleton Place, Ont.

–Carleton University (Ottawa)

–Carleton Village, N.S.

–*but* Carlton, Sask.

–Carlton Street (Toronto)

–Ritz-Carlton Hotel

carmaker

carpet, carpet-bag, carpet-sweeper

Cartier, George-Etienne (1814-1873)

cartilage

cassette

catalogue (*not* catalog)

catch-22 (a dilemma from which there is no escape); Catch-22 (Joseph Heller's book)

category, Category 2

Caterpillar, a Cat (trademark for a tractor)

Catholic (*but* Roman Catholic on first reference), Catholicism (religion)

catholic (universal)

CAT scan (computerized axial tomography)

Cattle–Capitalize breed names derived from proper names except where usage has established the lowercase.

–Holstein-Friesian

–Jersey, Guernsey, Ayrshire

–shorthorn

Caucasian

cave in (*v.*), cave-in (*n.*)

CBC for Canadian Broadcasting Corp.

C

–CBC is acceptable in all references.

–CBC-TV, CBC Radio One, CBC Radio Two

CBS Inc. (formerly Columbia Broadcasting System Inc.)

–CBS is acceptable in all references

–CBS's coverage

Cdn ($1,200 Cdn)

CD-ROM (compact disc read-only memory); acceptable in all references

cease fire (*v.*), ceasefire (*n.*)

Ceausescu, Nicolae (Romanian leader, 1918-1989)

Celanese (trademark for acetate, nylon, polyester, rayon)

cell block (in jail)

cellophane, celluloid, cellulose

cellphone (cellular phone)

Celsius, –30 C (dash, space before C, no period; specify Celsius only to avoid confusion)

cement (powder; used in concrete)

cemetery, Ocean View Cemetery

census, censuses

Centennial Year, the Centennial (1967)

–*but* Canada's centennial

–centennial celebrations

centimetre (cm — *sing.* and *pl.* metric symbol, no period)

Central Canada (Ontario and Quebec)

Central Committee

Centrale de l'enseignement du Quebec (Quebec teachers federation)

centre, centred, centring

–centre on (*not* around)

–centre field (baseball)

–centre-fielder

–centre-field wall

–John F. Kennedy Center for the Performing Arts

–Hummingbird Centre
–Rockefeller Center
Centre of Forensic Sciences (Toronto)
centurion (Roman soldier), Centurion (tank)
century, 20th century, second-century Rome
CFCs (chloro-fluorocarbons)
CF-18 (Canadian designation for the
   McDonnell Douglas aircraft)
chamber, lower chamber
  –Chamber of Deputies
  –Halifax Chamber of Commerce
  –the chamber of commerce
change-over (*n.*), change over (*v.*)
channel
  –Channel 10 (television)
  –English Channel and the Channel
  --Channel Tunnel (between Britain and France)
chaperon (*not* -one)
Chappaquiddick Island, Mass.
chapter (*no abbvn.*), Chapter 1
chargé(s) d'affaires, chargé d'affaires John
   O'Hara
charley horse
Charlottetown accord
Charter of Rights and Freedoms, the charter
chat room
check (restaurant bill)
check off (*v.*), checkoff (*n.*)
check up (*v.*), checkup (*n.*)
checker board, checkers, checkered flag
   (motor racing), checkered career
checkpoint (*one word*), Checkpoint Charlie
Chedabucto Bay, N.S.
cheddar cheese
chef-d'oeuvre, chefs-d'oeuvre
Chekhov, Anton (Russian writer, 1860-1904)
cheque (bank)
Chernomyrdin, Viktor (Russian politician)
cherub, cherubs

C

Chiang Kai-shek (1887-1975)
Chianti (wine)
chickenpox
chief
> –Chief Tom Whitefeather
> –police Chief Anna Myers
> –fire Chief Ron Espy

chief master sergeant
> –Chief Master Sgt. Phil McDonald

chief petty officer (*no abbvn.*)
chief warrant officer (*no abbvn.*)
childish (silly, puerile), childlike (innocent, trusting)
Children's Aid Society
Chile
chili, chilies
> –chili con carne
> –chili sauce

china (crockery)
China, People's Republic of (mainland, *but prefer simply* China)
Chinese (*not* Chinaman)
Chinese Names–Use the official Chinese spelling, Pinyin, for most personal and place names: Hua Guofeng (formerly Hua Kuofeng). Note that the family name (Hua) normally precedes the given name (Guofeng). But westernized Chinese often follow English practice: Robert Chow (*not* Chow Robert).
> Use the traditional spellings for well-known historical figures: Mao Tse-tung, Chou En-lai, and for Canton, Shanghai, Tibet.

chinook
Chipewyan (aboriginal band)
chisel, chiselled, chiseller
chlorophyll
choose, chose, chosen, choosing, choosy
Chornobyl (Ukraine)

Chou En-lai (1898-1976)

Chrétien, Jean

Christie's (auctioneer)

Christmas Day, Eve

chromosome

CHUM Ltd.

Church–Capitalize in names of religions and
      buildings.
        –Roman Catholic Church, Catholic
        Church (denomination)
        –St. Bartholomew's Church (building)
        –a church building

Church of Christ, Scientist (Christian Science Church
      acceptable in first reference)

Church of Jesus Christ of Latter-day Saints
      (Mormons)

chute (sluice, slide, parachute)

chutzpah (gall, audacity)

CIBC, Canadian Imperial Bank of Commerce

cigarette

cipher (*not* cypher)

circle (Circ.)

Circle, Arctic
      –but arctic winds, temperatures

Cirque du soleil

cirrhosis

citizens band (CB, *but avoid*)
      –citizens-band radio (*hyphen*)

city, city council
      –city hall (administration)
      –City Hall (building)
      –City of Halifax (corp.)
      –*but* in the city of Halifax
      –Quebec City (Quebec in placelines)

Citytv (Toronto)
      –CityPulse
      –CablePulse 24

Civil Aeronautics Board (U.S.)

Civil Service Commission (*no abbvn.*)

C

civil war
>–Spanish Civil War
>–Civil War (U.S.)

clamour

clangour (*but* clangorous)

Clarica Life Insurance Co.

Claridge's (London hotel)

Clark, Joe (politician)

Clarke, Austin (novelist)

Clarkson, Adrienne

Class–Lowercase school classes, except
>languages.
>–class of '61
>–mathematics class
>–French class

class (military)
>–S-class submarine
>–tribal-class destroyer

clean up (*v.*), cleanup (*n.*)

clear cut (*v.*), clearcut (*n.*)

Clearnet Communications Inc.

cliché

clientele

climactic (of a climax), climatic (of climate)

cloverleaf (on highways), cloverleafs

Club–Capitalize names.
>–Rotary Club
>–a club officer

CN–*See Canadian National*

CN Tower (Toronto)

co- (prefix), coadjutor, co-author (*n. only*),
>coaxial, co-chairman, coed, coexist,
>co-host (*n. only*), co-operate, co-ordinate,
>co-owner, co-pilot (*n. only*), co-worker.

coast
>–East Coast, West Coast, Gulf Coast
>(regions), B.C. coast, Atlantic coast
>(shorelines)

Coastal Command

coast guard
–Canadian Coast Guard
–U.S. Coast Guard
–the coast guard ship
–but coastguardman
cobalt-60
Cobol (common business oriented language)
Cobourg, Ont.
Coca-Cola, Coke (trademarks for cola drink)
coccus, cocci
cockney
coconut
–Cocoanut Grove (nightclub)
Codco (comedy TV)
code, city building code
–Criminal Code, the code
–Morse code
Cogeco Cable Inc.
cognoscente (*sing.*), cognoscenti (*pl.*)
coho (salmon — *sing.* and *pl.*)
Coke (as trade name for Coca-Cola)
Cold War
Colisée (Quebec City arena)
collectible(s)
College–Capitalize the names of
universities and colleges.
–McGill University
–University of Toronto (U of T)
–Victoria College
College Degrees–*See University Degrees*
College of Cardinals
collegiate, collegiate board, York collegiate
Collenette, David
Collins Bay, Ont.
–Collins Bay Penitentiary
Colombia (South America)
Colombo Plan
colonel (Col. Eric Anderson)
colour

Colorado (Colo.)

Colosseum (Rome)

Colville, Alex (painter)

Comaneci, Nadia (former gymnast)

combat, combated, combatant

come back (*v.*), comeback (*n.*)

Come By Chance, Nfld.

command, Maritime Command

commander (Cmdr. Wayne Elder)
>–lieutenant-commander (Lt.-Cmdr.)
>–wing commander (Wing Cmdr.)

commander of the Order of the British Empire
>(CBE)

commander-in-chief

commandment
>–the Ten Commandments
>–the Tenth Commandment

commando, commandos

command sergeant major
>–Command Sgt. Maj. Claude Laporte

commensurate

commiserate

Commission–Capitalize the proper name of
>government and royal commissions.
>–Canadian Transport Commission
>*but* the transport commission
>–Royal Commission on Newspapers
>*but* the newspapers commission

commitment

committal

committee
>–Commons finance committee

commodore (*no abbvn.*)

Common Prayer, Book of

common sense, a common-sense approach

Commons, House of
>–the House, the Commons

commonwealth
>–the Commonwealth

–Commonwealth of Australia
–Commonwealth Development Bank
–Commonwealth Games, the Games
–Co-operative Commonwealth
Federation (CCF)

communion, holy communion
–Anglican communion

communism (philosophical attitude)

Communist (party, government or member)
–anti-communist, non-communist,
pro-communist

communist ideals (philosophical)

Company–Use Co. in business names.
–American Broadcasting Cos. (ABC)
–Brown Co.
–*but* Canadian Opera Company
(entertainment)
–B Company (military)

company quartermaster-sergeant (*no abbvn.*)

company sergeant major (Company Sgt. Maj.
John Jones)
–company sergeants major

compare to (liken to), compare with (check
similarities and differences)

compatible

compel, compelled, compelling

competent (*not* -ant)

complementary (serving to complete),
complimentary (expressing compliment; free)

CompuServe

Computer terms–*See Internet*

concede

concept, conception
–Immaculate Conception

concerto, concertos

Concorde (aircraft)

condole, condolence (*not* -ance)

confectionery (*not* -ary)

Confederation (Canada)

C

 –Fathers of Confederation
Confederation of National Trade Unions
 (CNTU); in French, Conseil des syndicats
 nationaux (CSN)
conference
 –federal-provincial conference
 –Canada Conference (Evangelical)
 –Duke of Edinburgh's Study Conference
 –Law of the Sea conference
 –Conference Board of Canada
Conference on Security and Co-operation in
 Europe (CSCE, *but avoid*)
confidant (man), confidante (woman)
Confucian
Congo (formerly Zaire)
Congo-Brazzaville (formerly Republic of Congo)
congregation
 –Congregation of the Holy Office
 (Vatican)
Congress (U.S.)
 –*but* congressman, congressional
 –Senator John Smith (R — Tex.)
 –Representative Mary Smith (D — Mass.)
 –Congress party (India)
Congress of Racial Equality (CORE)
Connecticut (Conn.)
connoisseur (-nn-)
Connors, Stompin' Tom (country singer)
conscientious
Conseil des syndicats nationaux (CSN); *but
 prefer* Confederation of National Trade
 Unions (CNTU)
consensus (*not* consensus of opinion)
constable (Const.)
 –Const. Maria Huang
 –a city constable
constitution, the French Constitution, the
 constitution; *but* the Constitution (capped
 in all references to Canada)

consulate, French Consulate, the consulate
consul general, Consul General Guy Tremblay
Consumers' Association of Canada
consumer price index (CPI, *but avoid*)
consummate
contact (*v.*, *adj.* and *n.*)
Contadora
Continent, the (Europe)
continental shelf
contralto, contraltos
controller (*no abbvn.*)
    –Controller Gillian Towers
convener (*not* -or)
converter (*not* -or)
cookbook
Coon Come, Matthew (Coon Come in
    second reference)
co-operate, co-operation
Co-operative Commonwealth Federation (CCF)
co-ordinate
copy editing, copy editor
copyright
    –Copyright, The Canadian Press
CORE (for Congress of Racial Equality)
co-respondent (divorce), correspondent
    (writer)
cornea (*sing.*), corneas (*pl.*)
Corner Brook, Nfld.
Corner Brook Western Star
cornerstone, lay
Cornwall Standard-Freeholder
corporal (Cpl. Jane Smith)
    –lance-corporal (Lance-Cpl.)
Corporation–Use Corp. in business names.
    –Eastman Kodak Corp.
    –British Broadcasting Corp. (BBC)
    –Canadian Broadcasting Corp. (*but* CBC
    preferred)
corral, corralled

C

Correctional Service of Canada, correctional service
cosy (*not* cozy)
council, city or county council, Peel regional council
> –Canada Council
> –Council of Canadian Filmmakers (*no
> hyphen, no abbvn.*)
> –Council of Maritime Premiers
> (organization)

Council for Yukon Indians (*not* of; CYI, *but avoid*)
councillor (Coun.)
> –Coun. Robert Jones
> –a city councillor

counsel, Crown counsel, Queen's counsel
> (QC)

counsellor
counter-attack, counter-proposal
countrywide
County–Capitalize when preceding or
> following a specific term.
> –Waterloo County
> –County Derry
> –*but* in the county of Waterloo

coureur de bois, coureurs de bois
Court–Capitalize superior courts but not
> lower courts.
> –Admiralty Court
> –Appeal Court
> –Court of Queen's Bench
> –European Court of Justice
> –family court
> –Federal Court
> –judicial committee of the Privy Council
> –Ontario court of justice (lower court)
> –provincial court
> –small claims court
> –Superior Court (Que.), Superior Court
> of Justice (Ontario)
> –Supreme Court (fed., prov., state)
> –youth court

C

–the court ordered

Courtenay, B.C.

courthouse, courtroom

court martial, courts martial (*n.*),
    court-martial (*v.*)

Court of St. James's

Covent Garden (*not* Gardens)

cover up (*v.*), coverup (*n.*)

CPR — *See Canadian Pacific*

craftman (*no abbvn.*)
    –Craftman Elwood Greene (military)
    –*but* craftsman (artisan)

crape (*n.*, black material for mourning), crapy (*adj.*)
    See crêpe

Crediter, Social (*not* -or); Socred is acceptable

creditor (one owed a debt; *not* -er)

Cree (*sing.* and *pl.*)

crêpe (crapy fabric), crêpe de Chine; crêpe
    (pancake); crêpe paper

crescent (Cres.)

Crete, Paul (politician)

cricket
    –England-Australia Test match
    –the Test
    –the Ashes

Crime Stoppers (*two words*)

Criminal Code, the code

crisis, crises

criterion, criteria

criticism, criticize (*not* -ise)

Croat(s) (*n.*), Croatian (*adj.*)

CROP (Centre de recherche sur l'opinion
    publique; Quebec polling organization)

cross-border

cross-checking

cross-country

cross-examine, cross-examination

crown
    –the Crown (judge or prosecutor)

C

    –the Crown alleges ...
    –Crown attorney, counsel
    –Crown attorney Liz Baker
    –a Crown corporation, Crown land
    –a crown prince
    –*but* Crown Prince Rupert

Crowsnest Pass
cruise (missile)
Crusades
crybaby (*no hyphen*), crybabies
CTV Newsnet
Cultural Revolution
cummings, e.e. (1894-1962)
cup, Stanley Cup (trophy)
    –America's Cup (yachting)
    –Canada Cup (hockey)
    –Canada's Cup (yachting)
cupful, cupfuls
Curia (Vatican office)
Curling–free-guard zone, in-turn draw,
    out-turn draw
curriculum, curricula
curtain, Iron Curtain
curtsy, curtsies
CUSO (OK in first reference, orginally stood for
    Canadian University Service Overseas)
customs, Canada Customs
    –a customs officer
    –go through customs
cyberspace
cyclosporine
cystic fibrosis
czar, Czar Nicholas
Czechoslovakia (former country now divided into
    Czech Republic and Slovakia)

D

dachshund
Dacotah, Man.
Dacron (trademark for polyester fibre)
Dahomey (Benin since 1975)
DaimlerChrysler
Dalai Lama, the
Dalmatian
Dalphond-Guiral, Madeleine (politician)
dame, Dame Joan Sutherland (Dame Joan or,
        preferably, Sutherland on second
        reference)
damn, damned, damn it, God damn
Dances–Lowercase names.
        –break dancing, bump, charleston,
        foxtrot, go-go, hip-hop, minuet, pas de
        deux, polka, polonaise, twist
danish (pastry)
Dar es Salaam
        –DAR ES SALAAM (in placelines)
Dark Ages
Dash 8
data (*plural*)
database
dateline, placeline
        –*but* international date line
Dates–Write December 1997 without commas;
        and Dec. 14, 1997, with commas. In dates
        abbreviate the months except March,
        April, May, June and July: Aug. 1, May 3.
        Write Christmas 1995.
        –1997-98 but 1999-2002
da Vinci — *See Leonardo*
Day–Capitalize religious holidays and feasts
        and all special times.
        –All Saints' Day
        –Christmas Eve
        –Apple Day
        –*but* election day
day care *but* day-care centre

D

daylight (*not* daylight saving) time
    ADT, EDT, etc.
day trader
D-Day (June 6, 1944)
DDT (dichlorodiphenyltrichloroethane)
de, der, di, du, d'–When lowercase in names,
    capitalize only at start of sentence.
    –deBues, Vera (YWCA)
    –de Cotret, Robert (politician)
    –de Gaulle, Charles
    –de Grandpré, A. Jean (businessman)
    –de Havilland Inc.
    (division of Bombardier Inc.)
    –De Laurentiis, Dino (movies)
    –deLorean, John (business)
    –deMille, Cecil B. (movies)
    –de Valera, Eamon
    –deWit, Willie (boxing)
    –de facto (two words — existing,
    whether legal or not)
    –de jure (two words — by right, by law;
    but avoid)
    –deluxe (*one word*)
    –de rigueur (*not* -geur)
de- (*prefix*)
    –deactivate, debar, decompress,
    de-emphasize, de-escalate, defrost,
    de-ice, de-ink, deodorize, de-salt,
    de-Stalinization
dean of arts
debacle
debonair
deceit, deceitful
deceive, deceivable (*not* -eable), deceiver
decision-making
-decker, double-decker
Decorations–Capitalize specific names.
    –Distinguished Service Cross (DSC)
decrepit

D

deductible (*not* -able)

deepsea (*adj., no hyphen*)

Deep South (U.S.)

defence (*not* defense), *but* defensive

defenceman (*one word*)

Defence Research Board (DRB, *but avoid*)

defuse (remove fuse), diffuse (spread)

Degrees–Lowercase college and other degrees
　　　unless abbreviated — *See University Degrees.*

de-icing

Delaware (Del.)

delicatessen

delta, Mekong River Delta

demagogue, demagogy (*not* -goguery)

demeanour

Democrat
　　　–Representative Mary Smith (D — Tex.)
　　　–Senator John Smith (R — Mass.)

Democratic party (U.S.)
　　　–New Democratic Party (NDP)
　　　–a New Democrat

Dene (pronounced Den'-neh)
　　　–Dene Nation (represents aboriginals in
　　　Northwest Territories)

Denendeh (western Arctic)

Deng Xiaoping, Deng

Departments–Capitalize national and provin-
　　　cial government departments. Lowercase
　　　municipal, school and business
　　　departments.
　　　–Health Canada
　　　–Department of National Defence
　　　–Defence Department
　　　–Department of Indian and Northern Affairs
　　　–Indian Affairs Department
　　Lowercase department in plural uses.
　　　–the Defence and Industry departments
　　Capitalize the proper-name element when
　　　standing alone and used as noun meaning the

53

D

department.

–She went to Defence from Industry.

–*but* Toronto parks department

–McGill history department

dependant (*n.*), dependent (*adj.*),
    dependence (*not* -ance)

deprecate (disapprove), depreciate (belittle,
    lose value)

Depression (or Great Depression), the (1930s)

deputy

–Deputy Prime Minister Linda Graves
    (formal title)

–deputy premier Saul Hillier (informal
    position)

–deputy Speaker Jean Turcotte

–the deputy Speaker

–deputy Crown attorney Alys Yamata

de rigueur (*not* riguer)

de Savoye, Pierre (politician)

descendant (offspring)

descendent (descending)

-designate, prime minister-designate John
    Block, the chairman-designate

desirable (*not* -eable)

Desjarlais, Bev (politician)

desperate, desperation

despoliation (*not* despoilation)

detective

–Det. Fred Lisak (police)

–private detective James Brown

deterrent (*not* -ant)

Deutsche Grammophon (recordings)

Deutschmark (*prefer* German mark)

Devoir, Le (Montreal newspaper)

devotee

DEW (for Distant Early Warning) Line

Dhaka, Bangladesh

Dhaliwal, Herb (politician)

diagnose, diagnosis

dialysis

diameter

Diana, or Princess of Wales (*not* Princess
 Diana)

diaphragm

diarrhea

DiCaprio, Leonardo (actor)

Dickensian

Dictaphone (trademark for a dictation
 recorder)

die, dying

Diefenbaker, John

diesel engine (*lowercase*)

Diet (national legislative body)

dietitian

diffuse (spread), defuse (remove fuse)

dike (barrier; *not* dyke)

dilemma

dilettante, dilettantes

DiMaggio, Joe (1914-1999)

dining room

diocese, Hamilton diocese

Dion, Stéphane

diphtheria

diphthong

disappoint

disaster, disastrous

disc, compact disc (CD, CD-ROM), slipped disc, disc
 brake, disc jockey *but* floppy disk, diskette

discernible (*not* -able)

discolour

Discovery Channel, the

discreet (circumspect), discrete (separate, abstract)

disease, legionnaires' disease, Minamata disease

dishonour

disingenuous (insincere)

disinterested (impartial), uninterested (*not*
 interested)

dispatch (*not* despatch)

       –dispatch rider

       –mention in dispatches

       –a news dispatch

dispel, dispelled

dissension (*not* -tion)

dissociate (*not* disassociate)

distil, distiller

Distinguished Service Cross (DSC)

Ditto (trademark for copier)

dived (*not* dove)

divisibility, divisible, divisive

division, 6th Division

divorcée (woman, *but avoid*)

DJ (*not* deejay)

DNA (deoxyribonucleic acid)

doctor (Dr., *but avoid* unless health care
       professional)

       –doctor of laws (LLD)

       –doctor of medicine (MD)

       –doctor of philosophy (PhD)

docudrama

Dofasco Inc. (formerly Dominion Foundries
       and Steel Corp.)

dogcatcher, dogfight, doghouse, dog-tag

dogma, dogmas

Dogs–Capitalize breed names derived from
       proper names except where usage has
       established the lowercase.

       –Dalmatian

       –Doberman pinscher

       –German shepherd

       –Newfoundland, Great Dane

       –St. Bernard, Irish terrier

       –*but* alsatian, dachshund, collie,
       pekinese, spaniel, etc.

Dominica (small Caribbean island republic)

Dominican Republic (neighbour of Haiti)

dominion

       –Dominion of Canada

domino, dominoes
Domtar Inc.
donegal tweed
    but County Donegal
donkey, donkeys
Donnybrook (town), donnybrook (riot)
dos and don'ts
Dosanjh, Ujjal (B.C. premier)
Dostoyevsky, Fyodor (novelist, 1821-1881)
dot-com (company, millionaire, etc.)
double-A-plus, double-A-minus (bonds)
doublecross, doublecrosser
double-decker
doubleheader (*one word*)
doubletalk
doughnut (*never* donut except in corporate names)
Doukhobor
Dow Jones (*no hyphen*)
    –Canadian Dow Jones Ltd.
Down East
downhill
down payment (*two words*)
Down syndrome
    –Down Syndrome Association of
    Canada
Down Under (Australia and New Zealand)
D'Oyly Carte
draconian
draegerman (mine-rescue worker)
draft (air, money, plan, military, hauling,
    beer)
draftsman
Dragon (sailboat)
Dramamine (trademark for travel-sickness medicine)
dreck
dressing room (*two words*)
drive (Dr.)
    –111 Sutherland Dr.
    –*but* 24 Sussex Drive (official residence)

D

drive in (*v.*), drive-in (*n.*)
Droit, Le (Ottawa-Hull newspaper)
drop out (*v.*), dropout (*n.*)
drugstore (*one word*)
dry, drier, driest
    —*but* hair, laundry dryer
Dubai
duchess, Duchess of Windsor
Duesseldorf, Germany
duffel bag, coat
duke, Duke of Windsor
dumbfound
Dunkirk (*not* Dunkerque)
Dunlap, David Dunlap Observatory (near
    Toronto)
DuPont Canada Inc.
    —E. I. du Pont de Nemours and Co.
    —Irénée du Pont
    —Samuel F. Du Pont (his usage)
durum wheat
Dutoit, Charles (conductor)
DVD (for digital video disc; OK in first reference)
dwarf, dwarfs
dye, dyeing
dynamo, dynamos
dysentery
dysfunction
dyslexia

earl, Earl Baldwin
    –Earl of Athlone
Earle, Gordon (politician)
Earth–Capitalize when referred to as a planet.
    –The planets nearest the sun are
    Mercury, Venus and Earth.
    –The astronauts turned back to Earth.
    –down to earth
    –the good earth
    –heaven on earth
East–Capitalize regions *but not* their
    derivatives. Lowercase mere direction or
    position.
    –the East (region)
    –an easterner
    –Eastern Canada
    –an eastern Canadian
    –eastern Canadian markets
    –The snow moved east over Eastern
    Canada.
    –in eastern Quebec
    –East Coast (region)
    –east coast (shoreline)
    –where East meets West
    –eastern nations
    –eastern Europe (no longer a bloc)
    –Eastern Hemisphere
    –the Far East
East Block (Ottawa)
Eastern Townships (Quebec)
Eatons (division of Sears Canada Inc.)
EBay (*not* eBay)
Ebola virus
echo, echoes
E. coli (bacteria)
e-commerce (*prefer* electronic commerce,
    Internet commerce)
Economic Council of Canada

E

ecstasy (*lowercase*) (OK in first reference for
    methylenedioxymethamphetamine)

ecumenical council

eczema

Edmundston, N.B.

EDT (*not* EDST)

educator (*prefer* teacher)

effect (*n.* — result); (*v.* — bring about)

effrontery (shameless insolence), affront
    (deliberate insult)

e.g. (exempli gratia; *avoid*)

Eggleton, Art (politician)

Eglin (*not* Elgin) Field, Fla.

Eiffel Tower (Paris)

Eilat (Israeli port)

Einstein, Albert (1879-1955)

El ("the")–In Arabic names, lowercase when
    full names used, capitalize when first
    name dropped.
        –Thami el Glaoui *but* El Glaoui
        –El'Arish

-elect, president-elect Bill Clinton
        –*but* prime minister-designate Jean Chrétien

election day

Elections Canada

Elizabeth Fry Society

Elliot Lake, Ont. (*one t*)

ellipsis, ellipses

Elysée Palace

e-mail, electronic mail

embargo, embargoes

embarrass, embarrassment

embassy, Canadian Embassy, Ukrainian Embassy,
    the embassy

embryo, embryos

emeritus
        –Jean Duval, professor emeritus of
    history

emigrant, emigrate, emigration

Emmy, Emmys (TV awards)

emphysema

empire

      –British Commonwealth and Empire, the
      Empire

      –Holy Roman Empire

Empire State Building

enamour, enamoured (of)

encyclopedia

      – *but* Encyclopaedia Britannica

endeavour

Energy Board, National (NEB, *but avoid*)

Engel, Marian (writer, 1933-1985)

England–Do not abbreviate and do not use as
      synonym for Britain.

English Canada, English-Canadian

enormity (wickedness), enormousness (size)

Enquirer, Cincinnati (newspaper)

enquiry — *Use* inquiry

enrol (*not* enroll), enrolled, enrolment

en route (*always two words*)

ensign (rank, *no abbvn.*)

ensign, the Red Ensign

ensure (make sure of)

entomological, entomologist, entomology

entrepreneur, entrepreneurial

Environmental Protection Agency (EPA, *but avoid*)

epigram (witty saying), epitaph (inscription
      on a tomb), epithet (descriptive word or phrase)

equator

Erasmus, Georges

Erickson, Arthur (architect)

Ericsson, Leif (Viking)

erratum, errata

Eskasoni (Cape Breton First Nations band)

esker (post-glacial gravel)

Eskimo, Eskimos, *but use* Inuk, Inuit

Eskimo Point (*see Arviat, Nunavut*)

Esquimalt, B.C.

E

esthete, esthetic

Eternal City

eucharist (holy communion)

euphemism (pleasant word for an unpleasant subject), euphuism (flowery writing)

euro(s) (European Community currency)

Eurodollar (*no hyphen*)

European Court of Justice

European Parliament (legislative body of EU)

European Union (EU)

euthanasia (*preferred to* mercy killing)

even-steven

everyday (*adj., one word*)

exaggerate, exaggeration

exhilarate

exhort

existence (*not* -ance)

exonerate

exorbitant (*not* exhorbitant)

expedite, expediter (*not* -or)

expel, expelled

Expo 67, Expo 86 (*no apostrophe*)

extemporaneous (*not* -eraneous)

extra-bill (*v.*), extra billing (*n.*)

extracurricular

extrapolate (*not* exterpolate)

extraterritorial (*no hyphen*)

extravagant (*not* -ent)

extravaganza

exuberant

Exxon Corp.

eye, eyeball, eyebrow, eyeful, eyeing, eyelash, eyelid, eyesight, eyesore, eyewitness (*no hyphens*)

e-zine (Internet magazine)

face off (*v.*), faceoff (*n.*)
faculty, faculty of law
FA Cup (Football Association Cup)
    –the Cup competition
Fahd Ibn Abdul Aziz
    –King Fahd (Saudi Arabia)
Fahrenheit, –20 F (dash, space before F, no
    period)
Fairbairn, Joyce (senator)
Falconbridge Ltd.
fall (season)
fallacious, fallacy
fallible, fallibility
Fallopian tube
fall out (*v.*), fallout (*n.*)
fantasy
Far East
Far North
Farquharson, Charlie (TV character)
fascism (philosophical attitude)
Fascist (party, member or government)
fascist trends
Father's Day (third Sunday in June)
Fathers of Confederation
faux pas
favour, favourite, favourable
fax (*n.* and *v.*)
faze (disconcert), phase (stage)
federal
    –federal election
    –federal government
Federal Bureau of Investigation (FBI)
Federal Communications Commission (FCC, *but avoid*)
Federal Court
Federal Energy Administration (FEA, *but avoid*)
Federation of Canadian Municipalities (*no abbvn.*)
feedback (*n., no hyphen*)
feisty
fellow, fellowship

        —a Southam Fellow

        —Nieman Fellowship

ferris wheel (*lowercase*)

fervour

Fête nationale (Quebec holiday on June 24,
        also St-Jean-Baptiste Day)

fettuccine

fetus (*not* foetus)

Feux follets, the (*no hyphen* — dance group)

fever, Lassa fever, spring fever

Fiberglas (trademark for fibreglass or glass
        fibre)

field, a polo field

        —Soldier Field

field marshal (*no abbvn.*)

fiery, fierier, fieriest

Fife wheat, Red Fife wheat

Fifth Estate, The (TV program)

Fig Newton (trademark for cookies)

fighter-bomber

Filion, Hervé (harness racing)

Filipino (male), Filipina (female), Filipinos

film, filmmaker

        —Council of Canadian Filmmakers (*no abbvn.*)

fiord

fire, fire department, firearm, firebrand, firebomb
        firecracker, firefighter, fireplace

first lady (U.S. president's wife, *but avoid*)

first lieutenant (1st Lieut.)

First Nations

First World War (*not* World War I)

fivepins (bowling)

flack (press agent), flak (anti-aircraft fire)

Flags–Capitalize the names of flags and ensigns.

        —Fleur-de-lis, Maple Leaf, Red Ensign,
        Rising Sun, Stars and Stripes, Tricolour, Union Jack

flair (talent), flare (flame, widening)

flak (anti-aircraft fire), flack (press agent)

flamboyant (*no* u)

flamingo, flamingos
flammable (*prefer to* inflammable)
flare up (*v.*), flare-up (*n.*)
flatcar
flaunt (show off), flout (mock)
flavour
fleet
       –the U.S. fleet (whole navy)
       –U.S. Pacific Fleet (formation)
       –Fleet Air Arm (Royal Navy)
Fleming, Sir Sandford (1827-1915)
fleur-de-lis (*not* -lys), Fleur-de-lis (flag)
flexibility, flexible
flight lieutenant (Flight Lieut.)
flight sergeant (Flight Sgt.)
floe (floating sheet of ice)
Florida (Fla.)
flotation (*not* float-)
flounder (thrash about), founder (sink)
flout (mock), flaunt (show off)
FLQ (Front de libération du Québec)
flu (*no apostrophe*)
fluorite (mineral), fluorescence, fluoride,
       fluorocarbon, fluoroscope
flutist
flyer (*not* flier), fly-fishing, flyleaf, flypast,
       fly swatter (*two words*), flyweight,
       flywheel, frequent flyer
Flying Dutchman (sailboat)
flying officer (*no abbvn.*)
FM (frequency modulation)
FN (for Fabrique nationale) rifle
focus, focused, focuses, focusing
folksinger, folksong
followup (*n.* and *adj.*)
Fonteyn, Dame Margot
Food and Agriculture Organization of the
       United Nations (FAO)
foofaraw

F

foot-and-mouth disease (*not* hoof-)

Football–backup centre, ball carrier, ball club,
blitz (*n.*, *v.*), bootleg, end line, end zone,
field goal, fourth-and-one (*adj.*), fullback,
goal line, goal-line stand, halfback,
halftime, handoff, kick off (*v.*), kickoff
(*n.*, *adj.*), left guard, linebacker, lineman,
nose tackle, out of bounds (*adv.*), out-of-
bounds (*adj.*), pitchout (*n.*), place kick,
placekicker, play off (*v.*), playoff (*n.*, *adj.*),
quarterback, runback (*n.*), running back,
tailback, tight end, touchback,
touchdown

forbear (refrain from), forbearance; forebear
(ancestor)

force-feeding

Forces, the; Canadian Armed Forces; Armed
Forces (capped for Canadian only)

forego (precede), foregone; forgo (go
without), forgone

Foreign Legion

Foreign Office (U.K.)

forerunner

foresaw, foresee, foreseeable, foreseen

foreword (in a book)

forfeit, forfeiture

forgivable (*not* -eable), forgive

forgo (go without), forgone; forego (precede),
foregone

format

former

–former King (of the U.K.)
–former king (other nations)
–former president George Bush
–former prime minister Brian Mulroney
–former Speaker John Fraser
–former senator Robert de Cotret

Formica (trademark for a laminated plastic)

formula, formulas

F

Formula One (auto racing)
Forrester, Maureen (contralto)
forsake, forsaken
Fort Chimo, Que. — *See Kuujjuaq*
Fort Chipewyan, Alta.
Fort Frances, Ont.
Fort Macleod, Alta.
Fort McMurray, Alta.
Fort Qu'Appelle, Sask.
Fortran (for formula translation)
founder (sink), flounder (thrash about)
Fourth Estate (press)
Fourth of July, July Fourth (U.S. holiday)
foxtrot (*one word*)
fracas
francization (*not* -isation — *but preferably
        avoid*)
Franco-Manitoban
Franco-Ontarian
francophone (*lowercase*)
Francophonie, la (French-speaking equivalent of the
        Commonwealth)
freebie (free trip or other benefit)
freelance (*n.*, *v.* and *adj.*); freelancer (*n.*)
Freemason (*one word*)
freestyle swimming
french bread, french door, french fries,
        french-fried potatoes
French Canada, French-Canadian
        –French-speaking Canadian
French Revolution
frequency modulation (FM)
fresco, frescoes
Freudian
Friedan, Betty (feminist)
Frigidaire (trademark for appliances)
Frisbee (trade name)
Frobisher Bay — *See Iqaluit, Nunavut.*
Front, the (off Newfoundland)

F

Front de libération du Québec (FLQ)
front-runner
Fry, Elizabeth Fry Society
Fry, Hedy (politician)
Frye, Northrop (scholar, 1912-1991)
FTP (for file transfer protocol)
Fudgsicle (trademark)
fuel, fuelled, fuelling, fuel cell, fuel injection
Fuehrer, the (leader; used by Adolf Hitler)
-ful, boxful, careful, cheerful, cupful(s),
      handful(s), harmful, spoonful(s),
      thoughtful, useful
fulfil (*not* fulfill), fulfilled, fulfilment
full time, a full-time job, working full time
fulsome (pejorative term, meaning excessive)
fundraiser, fundraising, fundraise
fungus, fungi
furor (*not* furore)
fusilier (*no abbvn.*)
      –Fusilier Georges Coté
futile, futilely, futility

gadget, gadgetry

Gadhafi, Moammar

gaff (spar; fish-landing stick); gaffe (faux pas)

Gagliano, Alfonso (politician)

Gagnon, Christiane (politician)

gaiety

Gallup poll

Gandhi (*not* Ghandi)

gardener

garnishee (*v.* — preferable to garnish)

Gap (store)

Gastown (in downtown Vancouver)

GATT (General Agreement on Tariffs and Trade)

gaucho, gauchos

gauge

gauntlet (*not* gantlet)

gefilte fish

geiger counter

Geiger-Torel, Herman (opera)

genealogist

general (Gen.)
>   –chief of the general staff
>   –Gen. Charles de Gaulle
>   –Gen. William Worth

General–In compounds, hyphenate general
>   when it is the key word: major-general.
>   Otherwise: attorney general, auditor general,
>   governor general, secretary general.

General Agreement on Tariffs and Trade
>   (GATT)

General Assembly (of UN)
>   –*but* general assembly of the United
>   Church

generation X, generation Xers

Genie (movie award)

genius, geniuses

gentile

genus, genera

Geographical Terms–Capitalize regions but not

mere direction or position. Capitalize Lake, River, Mountain, Strait, County, etc., when preceding or following the specific term; *but* lowercase the common-noun part of names in plural uses: Ottawa and St. Lawrence rivers, lakes Huron and Superior.

George Cross (GC), Medal (GM)

George Weston Ltd.

Georges Bank (fishing)

George Town (Bahamas, Malaysia, Tasmania
    —most others Georgetown, *but* check)

Georgia (Ga.)

germane

German measles

Germany, Germanys

Gerussi, Bruno (actor, 1928-1995)

get together (*v.*), get-together (*n.*)

Ghanaian

ghetto, ghettos

ghoul, ghoulish

Gielgud, Sir John (actor, 1904-2000)

gigahertz (GHz; *avoid or include
    explanation*: one billion cycles a second)

gigolo, gigolos

Gillespie, Alastair

Girard-Bujold, Jocelyne (politician)

girlfriend, boyfriend

Girl Guides of Canada (association)
        —a girl guide, a guide
        —the Girl Guides, the Guides
        (association)
        —the Girl Guides movement
        —Brownie
        —Spark

Gitxsan-Wet'suwet'en

Giuseppe (Italian for Joseph)

gizmo, gizmos

gladiolus, gladioli

glamour (*but* glamorous)

glasnost

Globe and Mail, the Globe and Mail
    –in bylines only, *uppercase* the:
      By Greg Keenan
      The Globe and Mail

GNP (gross national product)

goalkeeper (*one word*)

gobbledegook

god (idol)

God–Capitalize sacred names and the proper
      names and nicknames of the devil: God,
      Allah, Yahweh, the Almighty, the
      Father, Jesus Christ, the Son, the Lamb
      of God, the Saviour, our Lord, Holy Spirit,
      Trinity, the Prophet (Mohammed),
      Virgin Mary, Archangel Michael, Angel
      Gabriel, Satan, Lucifer, Old Nick, Father of Lies.
    Capitalize He, Him, His, Thou, Thee,
      Thine, You, Your in reference to the
      Deity. But lowercase who, whom,
      whose.

godchild, godfather, godmother

God damn, God damned (*not* goddam) — *Use
    with discretion.*

godsend

Gods Lake, Man.

Goebbels, Josef (1897-1945)

Goering, Hermann (1893-1946)

gofer

go-go

goitre

Golden Horseshoe (Oshawa to St. Catharines,
    Ont.)

Golf–birdie (one under par), bogey (one over
      par; bogeys, bogeyed), double bogey,
      triple-bogey 7, eagle (two under par),
      par 4, par-4 hole, three-wood, No. 3 wood,
      1 over par for the round, shot a 1-over-par 73,
      Bell Canadian Open golf tournament,

Canadian Professional Golfers'
Association (CPGA), the Canadian Tour,
du Maurier Classic, AT&T Canada Senior Open,
Ladies Professional Golf Association
(LPGA), Masters tournament, PGA
Tour, Royal Canadian Golf Association (RCGA)

gonif (thief; clever person; prankster)

gonorrhea

goodbye (*no hyphen*)

Good Friday

Good Samaritan

goodwill (*n.* and *adj.*)

GOP (U.S. Republican party, *but avoid*)

gorilla

gospel, the Four Gospels
    –the Gospels
    –the Gospel of St. Luke
    –the gospel truth
    –a gospel singer

got (*not* gotten)

Goteborg

Gothic (architectural style) *but* a gothic novel

GO Transit, GO train (for Government of
    Ontario)

Gould, Glenn (pianist, 1932-1982)

Gouzenko, Igor (Soviet defector, 1919-1982)

Government–Capitalize national legislative
    bodies, including some short forms.
    –House of Commons, Commons
    –House of Lords, Lords
    –House of Representatives, House
    –Bundestag, Diet, Knesset
   Lowercase provincial legislatures and their
    equivalents, county or city councils and
    boards of school trustees.
    –Manitoba legislature
    –Quebec national assembly
    –Toronto city council

governor, governor-in-council (cabinet)

　　　　–Gov. Julius Mason
　　　　–former governor Anne Lewcyk
　　　　–Bank of Canada governor Heather Boyd
Governor General–Capitalize in all references
　　　　to the Canadian incumbent; otherwise
　　　　only as a title preceding a name.
　　　　–Gov. Gen. Adrienne Clarkson
　　　　–the Governor General (Canada)
　　　　–the governor general (others)
　　　　–former governor general Ed Schreyer
　　　　–governors general (*pl.*)
　　　　–Governor General's Awards, Governor
　　　　General's Award for poetry
　　　　–Governor General's Horse Guards,
　　　　Governor General's Foot Guards
Grade 7 — Use numerals; *but* seventh grade
graffito, graffiti
Graham, Alasdair (senator)
Graham, Katharine (Washington Post)
Grain–Capitalize variety names generally
　　　　except where usage has established the
　　　　lowercase.
　　　　–Thatcher, Selkirk, Rescue
　　　　–*but* durum, garnet, Alberta red winter,
　　　　No. 1 northern
grain grower
grain handler
Grammy, Grammys (record awards)
Granada (Spanish city), Grenada (island in
　　　　the Caribbean)
Grand Canyon
Grand Centre, Alta.
granddaughter, great-granddaughter
Grande Prairie, Alta.
Grande Prairie Herald-Tribune
grand jury
grandmaster (bridge and chess)
Grand Prix racing
　　　　–Canadian Grand Prix auto race

G

Grands ballets canadiens, les; les Grands
grassroots (*one word*)
Gray, Herb, (politician)
Greater Toronto Area (Toronto and
        surrounding urban regions)
great-grandfather, great-grandmother
Great-West Lifeco Inc.
Green Berets
Greene, Graham (novelist)
Greene, Lorne (actor, 1915-1987)
Greenly Island
green movement (environmentalists); Green
        party
green paper (a tentative report of government
        proposals)
Greenpeace Foundation
        –Greenpeace V (vessel)
Greenwich Village
Greer, Germaine (feminist)
Grenada (island in the Caribbean), Granada
        (Spanish city)
Grenfell, Sir Wilfred (1865-1940)
Gretzky, Wayne
Grewal, Gurmant Singh (politician)
grey (colour)
Grey Cup (football)
Grey, Deborah (politician)
Grey, Earl (governor general, Grey Cup)
Grey, Earle (arts award)
Grey Panthers
grey whale
grippe
grisly (gruesome), grizzly (bear)
Grit (Liberal)
gross domestic product (GDP)
gross national product (GNP)
groundcrew (aviation — *one word*)
Groundhog Day (Feb. 2)
ground swell (*two words*)

group captain (Group Capt. Ed Moir)

Group of Seven (artists, countries), the G-7

grown-up (*n.* and *adj.*)

gruesome

GST (acceptable in first reference for goods and
     services tax)

guacamole

guardsman (*no abbvn.; but* coastguardman)

guerrilla

guide, a girl guide
     –Girl Guides of Canada (association)
     –the Guides

Guinness (stout)
     –Arthur Guinness, Son and Co. (Dublin)
     Ltd.
     –Guinness Book of Records

Guinness, Sir Alec (1914-2000)

Gulf Canada Resources Ltd.

Gulf of Aqaba

Gulf Stream

gun, Bren gun, Sten gun

gung-ho

gunner (*no abbvn.*)

gunnery sergeant (Gunnery Sgt.)

Guns–Rifles, pistols and other small arms
     are usually described in calibre,
     expressed in decimal fractions of an inch
     or in metric. The word calibre is not used
     with metric measurements. Shotguns are
     measured in gauge.
     –M-16 rifle, 75-mm gun, 12-gauge shot-
     gun, .410-bore shotgun, .45-calibre
     automatic, .30-30 rifle, .22-calibre rifle

gunship

gunwale

Gurkha (*not* Ghurka)

gurney

guttural (*not* -eral)

Gwich'in (aboriginal band)

G

gynecologist, gynecology
Gypsy, Gypsies (race of nomadic peoples; also
    called Roma)
    −*but* gypsy moth, gypsy cab
Gzowski, Peter (broadcaster)

H–Four words and their derivatives begin
with silent "h" — heir, honest, honour
and hour — requiring "an": an honest
man. Otherwise: a historic battle, a hotel.

Haagen-Dazs (ice cream)

habeas corpus (writ)

Habsburg (*not* Hapsburg) Empire

Hague, The

Haida (*sing.* and *pl.*)

Haidasz, Stanley (senator)

hail, hailstone, hailstorm

Hailey, Arthur (novelist)

hair's-breadth

hajj (Muslim pilgrimage)

hakapik (club used in seal hunt)

half, one-half
    –half a dozen
    –a half-dozen

half-, halfback, half-baked, half-hour,
half-mast, halftime, halftone (engraving),
halves (*pl.*), halfway, halfwit, halfwitted

half-mast (*preferred to* half-staff)

Halifax Chronicle-Herald

Halifax Daily News

Halifax Mail-Star

Haligonian (resident of Halifax)

hall, city hall, firehall
    –Massey Hall
    –Roy Thomson Hall

Hall of Fame

Halley's comet

Halloween (*no apostrophe*)

Hamburger Helper (trademark for dinner mix)

Hamilton (*specify if not Ontario*)

Hamilton Tiger-Cats (*but* Ticats)

handcuff (*v.*), handcuffs (*pl. n.*)

Handel, George Frideric (composer, 1685-1759)

handful, handfuls

handmade (*one word*), *but* home-made

H

H&R Block Ltd. (*no periods; no spaces*)
handshake (*no hyphen*)
hangar (aircraft), hanger (clothes, etc.)
Hanger, Art (politician)
Hannover, Germany
Hanukkah
Hapsburg — *Use Habsburg*
hara-kiri
harass, harassing, harassment
harbour, Victoria harbour
hard line, hardline policy, hardliner
harebrained
Hare Krishna, Hare Krishnas
HarperCollins Canada Ltd. (publishers)
Harper's Magazine
Harris, Lawren (painter, 1885-1970)
Harrods (London store)
Hart, Jim (politician)
Hart Memorial Trophy, Hart Trophy (hockey)
hat trick
Havel, Vaclav
Hawaii (*no abbvn.*), Hawaiian
Hawker Siddeley Canada Inc.
H-bomb
Headingley, Man.
Headlines – Capitalize first word only. The usual CP rules for
      text apply, with the following changes to help keep
      headlines short:
      Abbreviations: Allowed in all uses for all Canadian
         provinces and territories except Yukon and
         Nunavut. Other well-known abbreviations can be
         used (StatsCan for Statistics Canada, etc.) as a last
         resort if length is an issue.
      For numbers under 10, use numerals (8 instead of
         eight).
      Symbols: Use % instead of per cent. Use M for
         million, but only after a numeral ($2M in fund
         ing). Q1, Q2, etc., permitted for first quarter,
         second quarter in business headlines.

Quotation marks: Use single, not double marks.
Capitalize the first word only, unless headline is in
   body of story, when all principal words are
   capped.

headquarters (*usually takes a plural verb*)

Heads–Capitalize principal words in headings of tables,
   lists and other tabular matter.

health care (*n.*) health-care (*adj.*)

hearsay

hearse

heat wave (*two words*)

heaven

heavy water

Hec Crighton Trophy

Hegira, the (Mohammed's)

Heimlich manoeuvre

helix, helixes

hell

Hello (*not* Hello!) magazine

Hells Angels (*no apostrophe*)

helter-skelter

hemisphere
      –Western Hemisphere

hemophilia

hemorrhage

Hennessy, Jill (actor)

herculean (*lowercase*)

Her Majesty–*See His*

hero, heroes (*pl.*)

heyday (*no hyphen*)

Hezbollah (Party of God)

hiccup, hiccuped

hide-and-seek, hideaway, hideout

hieroglyph, hieroglyphs (*n.*); hieroglyphic
      (*adj.*), hieroglyphics (*n., pl.*)

High Arctic

highbrow (*no hyphen*)

high commissioner, High Commissioner Lauren Chow

high jinks

H

highlight (*no hyphen*)
high mass
highrise
high-tech
highway
>   –the highway to Paris
>   –Highway 27
>   –Trans-Canada Highway

Hill, the (informal for Parliament Hill)
hindrance
Hindu, Hinduism
hippie, hippies
hippopotamus, hippopotamuses
Hirsch, John (1930-1989)
His–Capitalize His in reference to the Deity,
>   His (or Her) Majesty, His (or Her) Royal
>   Highness, His Holiness, His Grace, His
>   Honour, His Lordship, His Worship. But
>   use such terms of address only in quotations.
>   –His Worship Mayor Phillips
>   –and His Worship said ...
>   –His Royal Highness, the Prince of Wales

Hispanic
historic (important or outstanding in history)
>   –historical (about history)
>   –a (*not* an) historical site

Historical Eras–Capitalize historical periods
>   and events, including widely recognized
>   popular names: Pliocene Epoch, Stone
>   Age, Iron Age, Exodus, Ming Dynasty,
>   Dark Ages, Middle Ages, Hundred
>   Years War, Renaissance, American Civil
>   War, Prohibition, Great Depression, Roaring
>   '20s, Dirty '30s, Beer Hall Putsch,
>   Holocaust, Atomic Age, Space Age, Me
>   Decade – *but* ice age (no single period)
>   –21st century

History Television (specialty TV channel))
hitchhike, hitchhiking (*no hyphen*)

H

Hitler, Adolf (*not* Adolph) (1889-1945)

HIV (for human immunodeficiency virus),
　　HIV-positive

Hnatyshyn, Ray (former governor general)

Ho Chi Minh (North Vietnam), Ho Chi Minh Trail

Hockey–blue-line, face off (*v.*), faceoff (*n.*,
　　adj.), goalie, goal-line, goal-mouth,
　　goalpost, goaltender, left-wing pass, left-
　　winger, play off (*v.*), playoff (*n., adj.*),
　　power play, power-play goal, red-line,
　　right-winger, short-handed (*adj.*), shut
　　out (*v.*), shutout (*n., adj.*), slapshot

hodgepodge (*no hyphen*)

Hoeppner, Jake (politician)

Hogtown (nickname for Toronto)

hold up (*v.*), holdup (*n.*)

hole, buttonhole, pigeonhole

Holidays–Capitalize religious holidays and
　　feasts and all special times: Christmas
　　Eve, New Year's Day, Father's Day,
　　Easter, Hanukkah, Yom Kippur.

Hollinger Inc.

Holocaust (murder by Nazis of six million
　　Jews)

Holt, Renfrew and Co. Ltd.
　　–*but* Holt Renfrew (no comma)

Holy Father (the Pope, *but avoid*)

Holy Land

Holy See (Vatican)

Holy Week

home, homebrew, homegrown, homemade,
　　homeowner, home page (*two words*),
　　homesick, home town (*two words*),
　　home-town boy, homework

homey (*not* homy)

Hong Kong Special Administrative Region,
　　People's Republic of China (formal name,
　　Hong Kong *OK in all references*)
　　– Hongkong Bank of Canada (*one word*)

H

honky-tonk (*hyphen*)
honour, honourable *but* honorary
hoof, hoofs
Hook of Holland
hoopla
Horse Racing–race card, racecourse, race
      horse, racetrack, raceway.
horseback (*one word*)
hospital, hospital commission
      –Shaughnessy Hospital
      –St. John's General Hospital
      –Hospital for Sick Children
      –Laval hospital commission
hot, hotbox, hotcake, hotdog, hotfoot,
      hothead, hothouse, hotline (show, *prefer*
      open-line), hotplate, hotrod, (all one
      word); *but* hot air, hot-blooded, hot cross
      bun, hot pants, hot potato, hot war, hot
      water
hotel
      –Royal York Hotel
      –Hotel Vancouver
      –a Vancouver hotel
House of Commons (Canadian and British)
      –the House, the Commons
      –the lower house (Commons)
      –House leader Jean Roy (federal)
      –the house (provincial)
      –house leader Jean Roy (provincial)
hovercraft
      –SRN-6 hovercraft
      –British Hovercraft Corp.
HTML (Hypertext Markup Language)
hubbub
Hudson Bay
Hudson's Bay Co., the Bay
Hudson's Hope, B.C.
hullabaloo
humdinger

humdrum (*no hyphen*)
humongous
humour *but* humorous, humorist
hurricane Hazel
Hush Puppies (trademark for casual shoes)
Hussein, Saddam
Hutterites
hydroelectric (*no hyphen*)
Hydro-Québec (*hyphen*)
hyperlink
hypocrisy, hypocrite
hypothesis, hypotheses
hysterectomy
Hyundai Auto Canada Inc.
    –Hyundai Corp. (parent company)

Iacocca, Lee
I-beam
ice age (*no single period*)
icebreaker (*no hyphen*)
ice cream, ice-cream bar
icewine (*one word*)
Idaho (*no abbvn.*)
idiosyncrasy
i.e. (*but prefe*r that is)
Ignatieff, Michael (author)
Iles de la Madeleine
ill, ill feeling, ill will; *but* ill-fated,
         ill-mannered, ill-starred
Illecillewaet, B.C.
Illinois (Ill.)
illusion (false impression), allusion
         (indirect reference)
Imax (big-screen movies)
imitator (*not* -er)
immanent (pervading, inherent), imminent
         (impending)
immovable (*not* -eable)
imperial, imperial measure
Imperial Oil Ltd.
impetus, impetuses
implement (*n.* and *v.*), implementation
impostor (*not* -er)
impresario (*not* -ss-)
Impressionism (school of art)
         but impressionistic style
in, inbound, indoor, in-depth, infighting,
         in-group, in-house, in-law; break-in,
         cave-in, stand-in, walk-in, write-in
inaccessible (*not* -able)
inadmissible (*not* -able)
inadvertent (*not* -ant)
Inco Ltd. (formerly International Nickel Co.)
income tax
         –income tax deduction

I

incompatibility, incompatible

Incorporated–Use Inc. in business names.

incorruptible (*not* -able)

Independence Day (U.S.)

independent, Independent (MP), Ind (*abbvn.,
no period*)

in depth, in-depth (*adj.*)

index, indexes

Indiana (Ind.)

indict, indictable

indigenous

indispensable (*not* -ible)

Industrial Revolution

Indy-car race

infallible

infantry, 4th Infantry Battalion

infinitesimal

inflammable (*use* flammable)

inflammation, inflammatory

Infomart

information highway (*lowercase*)

Informetrica

infrared

ingenious (clever), ingenuous (frank, innocent)

in-line skating

inherent

innocuous

innovate, innovation, innovator

Innu (Labrador Indians)

innuendo, innuendoes

inoculate, inoculation

inquire, inquiry, inquiries
        – Cincinnati Enquirer
        – Philadelphia Inquirer

Inquisition, Spanish

inscribe (*not* enscribe), inscription

insignia (*sing.* and *pl.*)

insistence (*not* -ance), insistent (*not* -ant)

inspector, Insp. John Smith

install, installation
instalment
instil, instilled
institute
	–Women's Institute
insure (cover loss)
intefadeh (Palestinian uprising)
intelligence quotient (IQ)
Interac (banking)
Inter-American Development Bank
	(IDB, *but avoid*)
Inter American Press Association (IAPA, *but
	avoid*)
intercollegiate (*no hyphen*)
intercontinental (*no hyphen*)
inter-county (baseball)
interdependence (*no hyphen*)
interfere, interference
interferon (*lowercase*)
Interior, the (B.C.)
intern (hospital)
International Bank for Reconstruction and
	Development (World Bank)
International Civil Aviation Organization
	(ICAO)
International Court of Justice (*no abbvn.*)
international date line
International Development Association (IDA,
	but avoid)
International Grains Arrangement (*no
	abbvn.*)
International Joint Commission (IJC, *but
	avoid*)
International Labour Organization (ILO)
International Monetary Fund (IMF)
International Telecommunications Satellite
	Consortium (Intelsat OK in first reference)
International Telephone and Telegraph Corp.
	(now ITT Corp.)

I

International Wheat Agreement

Internet – Capitalize specific proper names.

> –Internet, the Net
>
> –World Wide Web, the Web, Web master, Web site
>
> –Adobe Acrobat, JavaScript

Lowercase descriptive or generic terms.

> –electronic mail, e-mail
>
> –chat room, cyberspace, domain name, home page, hyperlink, shareware

Use all caps for well-known acronyms.

> –CD-ROM, FTP, HTML, HTTP (but lowercase in Web addresses), RAM, URL

In Internet addresses, follow upper and lowercase of actual address.

> –sympatico.ca, globeandmail.com, www.cp.org, www.amazon.com, etc.

If the company uses a variation of its Internet address as its corporate name, capitalize the first word: Amazon.com.

interpreter (*not* -or)

interracial (*no hyphen*)

intervene, intervener (*not* -or)

Intracoastal Waterway (*not* Inter-)

intranet (*lowercase*)

Inuit Tapirisat (Inuit organization)

Inuk (*sing. n.* and *adj.*), Inuit (*pl. n.* and *adj.*)

Inuktitut (language)

inundate, inundation

Inuvialuit (western Arctic aboriginals)

Inuvik, N.W.T.

Investors Group Inc.

involvement

IODE (official name of Imperial Order Daughters of the Empire)

Iowa (*no abbvn.*)

Ipsco Inc. (Interprovincial Steel and Pipe Inc.)

Iqaluit, Nunavut

IRA (Irish Republican Army)

iridescent

Irish hospitals sweepstake
    –Irish Sweeps Derby
Irish Republican Army (IRA)
Iron Curtain (outmoded term)
ironic, ironically (use advisedly; often
    misused)
irrelevant
irreparable
irresistible (*not* -able)
irreverent (*not* -ant)
island
    –Vancouver Island
    –the Island (informal for Vancouver
    Island and P.E.I.)
Ismailia (*not* Ismailiya)
Ispat Sidbec Inc. (Quebec steel company)
Itar-Tass news agency
it's (it is, it has; similar to he's, she's)
    –its (possessive; similar to his, hers)
ITT Corp. (parent company)
    –ITT Canada Ltd.
IUD (acceptable on first reference for
    intra-uterine device)
Ivy League

o)

eak

)
e Jaycees
vehicle), Jeep (for the
ll-terrain vehicle)
ny (football)

Witnesses
a Jehovah's Witness, a Witness
k, Otto (politician)
-O (trademark for gelatin dessert)
jerry-built
Jet Ski (trademark for personal watercraft)
JetStar
Jew (for man and woman, not Jewess)
        —Reform Jew
        —Orthodox Jew
jeweller, jewelry
Jiang Zemin
        —Jiang (*second reference*)
Jidda, Saudi Arabia
jockey, jockeyed, jockeys
jodhpurs
john (lavatory; prostitute's customer)
Johns Hopkins Hospital, University
joual (Quebec dialect)
Journal de Montréal, Le (newspaper)
Journal de Quebéc, Le (newspaper)
Juan Carlos de Borbon
        —Juan Carlos I (king of Spain)
judge, Judge Catherine Tracy
judgment (*not* judgement)
Juilliard School of Music
jumbo jet (wide-bodied jet plane,

including the Boeing 747, Lockheed
L-1011 and DC-10)

junior
—John Jones Jr. (*no comma*)

Juno Awards, Junos

jury, grand jury

justice, Chief Justice Albert Weisman,
Justice Jean Dupont, Justice Sadie Kells (*not*
Madam Justice); Smith or the judge or
justice in second reference

justice of the peace
—justice of the peace Jean Dufy

K

Kaczynski, Theodore (unabomber)
kaffeeklatsch
Kahnawake (formerly Caughnawaga)
kaiser, Kaiser Wilhelm
kamikaze
Kampuchea (now Cambodia)
Kaposi's sarcoma (AIDS-related cancer)
Karadzic, Radovan
karat (gold), carat (gems)
Karsh, Yousuf (photographer)
Kathmandu
Kazakhstan
Kejimkujik National Park, N.S.
Kempston Darkes, Maureen (president GM Canada)
Kenora Miner and News
Kentucky (Ky.)
kerfuffle
ketchup
keynote (*no hyphen*)
Keystone Kops
KGB (acceptable in all references for the
        Russian words meaning Committee of
        State Security, *but* include a descriptive
        phrase such as former Soviet secret
        police)
Khachaturian, Aram (composer, 1903-1978)
Khadafy — *See Gadhafi*
khaki
Khan, Genghis (c. 1162-1227)
Khashoggi, Adnan (financier)
Khmer Rouge
Khomeini, Ayatollah Ruhollah (1902-1989)
Khrushchev, Nikita (1894-1971)
kibbutz (communal farm), kibbutzim (*pl.*),
        kibbutznik (resident)
kibitz, kibitzer
kick back (*v.*), kickback (*n.*), kick off (*v.*),
        kickoff (*n.*)
kidnap, kidnapped, kidnapper

K

Kiev – *Use* Kyiv
kilo (*not* an abbreviation for kilogram or kilometre)
kilometre (km — *sing.* and *pl.* metric symbol, *no period*)
 –km/h
Kimberley, B.C.
Kimberly-Clark Canada Ltd.
kimono, kimonos
kindergarten
King, William Lyon Mackenzie (1874-1950)
 (usually just Mackenzie King; King on
 second reference)
King (of the U.K.), king (other nations)
Kingston Whig-Standard
Kinsmen Clubs
Kitchener-Waterloo Record
kitsch
Kitty Litter (trademark for cat litter)
Kiwanis International
Kleenex (trademark for paper tissue)
klieg lights
Klondike
Kluane National Park
klutz (a bungler)
Kmart stores (*not* K-Mart)
km/h (kilometres per hour)
knick-knack (*hyphen*)
knight
 –Knights of Columbus
 –Knights of Pythias
know-how (*hyphen*)
knowledgeable
Kool-Aid
Kootenai River (U.S.)
Kootenay East, West (B.C. regions)
Kootenay River (B.C.)
Koran –*Use* Qur'an
Kostunica, Vojislav (Yugoslav politician)
Kosygin, Alexei (1904-1980)
Kouchibouguac National Park, N.B.

kowtow
Krakow, Poland
Krazy Glue (trademark for instant glue)
krebiozen (cancer drug)
Kreviazuk, Chantal (singer)
Krieghoff, Cornelius (1815-1872)
krona, kronur (Icelandic currency)
krona, kronor (Swedish currency)
krone, kroner (Danish and Norwegian currency)
kudos (always singular)
Kuerti, Anton (pianist)
Ku Klux Klan
kung fu
Kurelek, William (painter, 1927-1977)
Kuujjuaq, Que. (formerly Fort Chimo)
Kyiv (*not* Kiev)
Kyrgyzstan (formerly Kirghizia)

La, Le–When lowercase in names, capitalize
only at the start of the sentence. Prefer
"the" before French names of associations and groups; capitalize "le" or "la"
when it is the first word of the title of a
book, song, play and the like.

Labatt
–Labatt Brewing Co. Ltd. (in Canada)
–Labatt Breweries North America
–Labatt Brier (curling)
–Labatt (*not* Labatt's) announced
–Labatt's beer

label, labelled

labour *but* laborious

Labour Day (*not* Labor Day)

labour sympathizer (union)

Labour sympathizer (party)
–Labour party

Labrador retriever

Lac de Gras, N.W.T.

Lac la Biche, Alta.

Ladies' Home Journal

Laetrile (trademark for a derivative of
amygdalin)

Lake–Capitalize as part of a proper name:
Eels Lake, Lake Huron. Lowercase in
plural use: lakes Erie and Ontario, Eels
and Duck lakes.

Lake of the Woods, Ont.

Lake Shore Boulevard (Toronto)

lama (monk), llama (animal)

LaMarsh, Judy (1924-1980)

lambaste, lambaster, lambasting

Lamborghini

landmine (*one word*)

Land Rover (trademark for an all-terrain
vehicle)

lang, k.d.

L'Annonciation, Que.

L

laptop (computer)

largemouth (bass)

largesse

larva, larvae

laryngitis

larynx, larynxes

lasagna

laser (for light amplification by stimulated
emission of radiation)

Lassa fever

lasso, lassos

L'Assomption, Que.

Last Spike

Last Supper

Latin America (*no hyphen*)

laudable

Laundromat (trademark for public laundry)

Laurence, Margaret (author, 1926-1987)

Laurier, Sir Wilfrid (1841-1919)
    –Wilfrid Laurier University

Lavalin Group Inc.

law
    –Law of the Sea conference

lawsuit

Lay–This is an action word; it takes a direct
object: The gunman lays the rifle down,
is laying it down, laid it down, has laid
it down, had laid it down, will lay it
down.

lay off (*v.*), layoff (*n.*)

lead (*v.*), led, leading

Leader–Capitalize as a semi-official title when
used with the name of a political party
and directly preceding a name.
    –NDP Leader Susan Watson
    –*but* party leader Susan Watson
    –deputy leader Jean Roy
    –former Tory leader Joe Clark
    –House leader Herb Gray (federal)

–house leader Claude Littlefeathers
(provincial)

–Chinese leader Deng Xiaoping

leading seaman (*no abbvn.*)

league

    –League of Nations

    –National Hockey League (NHL)

    –American League (baseball)

    –Catholic Women's League

leap, leapfrog (*n.* and *v. — no hyphen*), leap
    year

Learjet (trademark)

LeBlanc, Romeo

le Carré, John (author)

Led Zeppelin

leery (*not* leary)

leeway

Left Bank (Paris)

left, left field, left-fielder, left wing, left-winger,
    left-field wall, left-handed pitcher,
    left-wing politician (*adj., hyphen*)

left-handed, left-hander (hyphens)

legation, Canadian Legation, the legation

Léger, Paul-Emile Cardinal; Léger or the
    cardinal on second reference

legion

    –Foreign Legion

    –Royal Canadian Legion

legionnaire

legionnaires' disease

Legislature–Capitalize national legislatures;
    lowercase others.

    –Parliament, House of Commons, Com-
    mons, House *but* lower house; Senate *but*
    upper house; Congress, House of
    Representatives, House; Chamber of
    Deputies, Chamber; Knesset, Bundestag,
    French National Assembly.

    –Quebec national assembly, Manitoba

legislature, Newfoundland house of
assembly; legislature, house.

leitmotif

lend, lent (*v.*), loan (*n.*)

lenience

Lent (season)

Leningrad – *Use* St. Petersburg

Leonardo da Vinci (1452-1519), Leonardo
(*not* da Vinci) on second reference

Leopard 1 (tank)

Lepreau, Point

lesbian (*lowercase*)

leukemia

Levi's (trademark for a brand of jeans)

Lhasa, Tibet

liaison

libel, libelled, libellous

liberal (philosophical attitude)
–a liberal education

Liberal (party or member)
–the Liberal party
–Liberal Party of Canada (formal name)

liberty, liberty boat, *but* Liberty ship
–Statue of Liberty
–the Liberty Bell

library, Toronto public library
–National Library

Libya, Libyan

licence (*n.*), license (*v.*)

licensed, licensee, licensing

Lie–This verb, meaning to recline or be
situated, does not take a direct object:
Trudeau lies in state, is lying in state,
lay in state, has lain in state, had lain in
state, will lie in state.

lie (*n.*), lie-detector

Liechtenstein

lieutenant (Lieut. *but* Lt.- as prefix in compounds: Lt.-Col.)

L

–second lieutenant (2nd Lieut. Anne Finlay)
lieutenant-colonel (Lt.-Col. John Smith)
      –lieutenant-colonels
lieutenant-commander (Lt.-Cmdr. Stan Lyubic)
lieutenant-general (Lt.-Gen. Lee Ward)
      –lieutenant-generals
lieutenant-governor, lieutenant-governors
      –Lt.-Gov. Carole Pelletier,
      the lieutenant-governor said ...
life (*prefix*), lifebelt, lifeboat, lifebuoy, life
      cycle, lifeguard, life-jacket, lifeless,
      lifelike, lifeline, lifelong, life-preserver,
      life-raft, life-size, lifespan, lifestyle, life-support
      system, lifetime, life-work
Life Saver (trademark for a brand of candy)
lightface (type)
light heavyweight
lighthouse, lightkeeper
light-year
likable (*not* -eable)
lime, lime-kiln (*hyphen*), limelight (*no hyphen*)
Limey (slang for British)
Limited–Use Ltd. and ltée (*lowercase, no
      period*) in business names.
linage (advertising), lineage (ancestry)
linchpin (*not* lynchpin)
Lincoln Center
line, line 2
lineage (ancestry), linage (number of lines)
lineman (football player), linesman (hockey official)
line up (*v.*), lineup (*n.*)
Lions Gate Bridge
Lions, Gulf of
Lion's Head, Ont.
Li Peng, Li (*second reference*)
liquefied natural gas (LNG)
liquefy, liquefier, liquefaction
liqueur
lira, lire (*pl.*)

L

listserv (e-mail)
Listuguj (Mi'kmaq band)
Liszt, Franz (1811-1886)
litre (l — *sing.* and *pl.* metric symbol, *no
        period*)
Little World Series (baseball)
livable (*not* -eable)
living room
LLD (doctor of laws, *but avoid*)
Lloyd Webber, Andrew (composer)
Lloyd's (insurance market, shipping
        information)
        –Lloyds Bank (no apostrophe)
loan (*n.*), lend, lent (*v.*)
loan shark (*n. only — two words*)
loath (unwilling), loathe (despise)
Loblaw Cos. Ltd.
        –Loblaw (corporate reference), a Loblaws store,
        Loblaws (store)
Local 14 (union)
Locations, Places, Sites–Capitalize the
        names of important buildings,
        residences, historical and battle sites,
        universities and colleges, hospitals and
        hotels. Capitalize Union Station, Grand
        Central Station as important buildings
        but not when known by name of railway
        or town: the Via Rail station, Leaside
        station. Lowercase county courthouse,
        city hall, post office. Capitalize the names
        of parks, gardens, playing fields and
        arenas.
locker-room
lock out (*v.*), lockout (*n.*)
lock up (*v.*), lockup (*n.*)
lodge, Orange Lodge
        –the lodge meeting
Loewen Group Inc.
London Free Press

L

long distance, a long-distance phone call
long house
Long Island Rail Road
long johns
longliner (fishing vessel)
long-range, a long-range forecast
long-standing, a long-standing rule
long-term (*adj.*)
longtime (*no hyphen*, compound modifier)
Longueuil, Que.
loonie (dollar coin), loony (insane), Looney
        Tunes (cartoons)
loophole (*no hyphen*)
looseleaf (*no hyphen*)
loran (for long-range air navigation system)
Lords, the (institution), lords (members),
        Lord's (cricket ground)
Lord Thomson of Fleet
L'Orignal, Ont.
Losier-Cool, Rose-Marie (senator)
Loto Canada (*no hyphen*)
Loto-Québec (*hyphen*)
Louisbourg, N.S.
        –Fortress of Louisbourg
Louisiana (La.)
Lou Marsh Trophy
lovable (*not* -eable)
lowbrow (*no hyphen*)
lowercase (*n., v.*)
lower house
Lower Mainland (B.C.)
Lower Town (Quebec or Ottawa)
LSD (acceptable in all references for lysergic
        acid diethylamide)
Luftwaffe
Lunenburg, N.S.
Lutz (figure-skating jump)
Luxembourg
luxury, luxurious

L

Lycra (trademark for spandex fibre)
Lyme disease

MA (master of arts)
   —a master's degree
Macau
Macdonald, Angus L. (Nova Scotia politician,
      1890-1954; Halifax bridge)
Macdonald-Cartier Freeway, Highway 401
Macdonald College
MacDonald, Flora
MacDonald, J.E.H. (painter, 1873-1932)
Macdonald, Sir John A. (1815-1891)
Macdonald, Man.
MacIsaac, Ashley
MacKay, Peter (politician)
mace (staff of office; club), mace-bearer
Mace (trademark for a paralysing spray)
MacEachen, Allan (politician)
MacGregor, Man.
machiavellian
machine-gun
      —submachine-gun
Macintosh (computer)
   —*but* McIntosh (apple)
Mackenzie, Alexander (1822-1892)
Mackenzie Highway, River, Valley
Mackenzie Financial Corp.
MacKenzie, Lewis
Mackenzie, William Lyon (patriot, 1795-1861;
      grandfather of William Lyon Mackenzie King)
mackinaw (cloth, heavy coat)
mackintosh (coat)
Mack Truck (trademark)
MacLaren, Roy
Maclean's magazine
MacLennan, Hugh (author, 1907-1990)
Macmillan Co. of Canada Ltd. (publisher)
MacMillan, Sir Ernest (1893-1973)
MacNeil, Rita (singer)
Macphail, Agnes (Canada's first woman MP, 1890-1954)
Macpherson, Kay (feminist, 1913-1999)

M

madam (polite form of address;
    brothel-keeper)
madame (French title of respect)
    –Madame Robert Duval (*no abbvn.*)
mademoiselle (*no abbvn.*)
Madonna (performer), the Madonna (mother of Jesus)
maelstrom
Mafia; Mafioso, Mafiosi (member, *sing.* and
    pl.)
Magazine–Capitalize when part of the actual title.
    –New York Times Magazine
    –Maclean's magazine
    –Time magazine
Magdalen Islands (*prefer* Iles de la Madeleine)
Magna Carta (*not* Charta)
Magnum (trademark for a cartridge), a .357-
    calibre Magnum revolver, a Colt Python
    .357 Magnum
mail-order catalogue (*hyphen*)
Maine (Me.)
mainframe
major (Maj. Alice Lajoie)
major-general (Maj.-Gen. Keith Adams),
    major-generals
make up (*v.*), makeup (*n.*)
malemute (dog)
Mallorca
mammogram, mammography (breast X-ray)
mandarin (civil servant); Mandarin (Chinese dialect)
manhattan (cocktail)
manhunt
manila paper
Manila, Philippines
mankind (*prefer* humanity)
manmade (*prefer* synthetic, manufactured)
manoeuvre
Man of the Year
man-of-war (warship)
    –Man o' War (racehorse)

M

mantel (fireplace)
mantle (cloak)
Manulife Financial Corp.
Mao Tse-tung, Mao (*second reference*)
maple leaf, leaves
     –Maple Leaf (flag, emblem)
     –Toronto Maple Leafs
Maple Leaf Foods Inc.
Maple Leaf Gardens
March (*no abbvn.*)
march past (*n.* and *v.*)
Mardi Gras
marijuana
marine, marine corps
     –U.S. Marine Corps
     –Royal Marines
     –the Marines (service)
     –a marine
     –Marine Capt. Robert Grey
     –a section of 20 marines
maritime
     –Maritime provinces, the Maritimes
     –New Brunswick, Nova Scotia, P.E.I.
     –The Atlantic provinces comprise the
      Maritimes and Newfoundland.
Maritime Employers Association (MEA, *but avoid*)
Maritime Telegraph and Telephone Co. Ltd.
     –MT and T or Maritime Tel and Tel
Mark III, Mark 46 (follow maker's style)
marketplace
Mark, Inky (politician)
Marks & Spencer
Marleau, Diane (politician)
marquess *but* Marquis of Queensberry rules
Marquis wheat
Marseille
marshal (*n.* and *v.*), marshalled, fire marshal,
     parade marshal
Marshall Plan

M

martini
Martyrs' Shrine (at Midland, Ont.)
Marxism, Marxist
Maryland (Md.)
MASH
mason (person who builds with stone)
Mason (member of Masonic order)
Masonite (a trademark for a brand of
        hardboard)
Mason jar
mass, low mass, high mass, requiem mass
Massachusetts (Mass.)
massasauga (rattlesnake)
Masse, Marcel (politician)
mastectomy
MasterCard
master corporal (Master Cpl. Pierre Charest)
masterful (domineering), mastery (skilful)
master of arts (MA), a master's degree
master seaman (*no abbvn.*)
master sergeant (Master Sgt.)
master warrant officer (*no abbvn.*)
matrix, matrixes
matzo, matzos
mavin (an expert)
maximum, maximums
mayday (distress signal)
mayonnaise
mayor, Mayor Grace McDonald
        –the mayor of Ottawa
        –former mayor Ken Elman
        –acting mayor Ken Elman
        –the acting mayor
        –mayor-elect Ken Elman
mayoralty (*n.*), mayoral (*adj.*)
Mazankowski, Don (politician)
mazel tov (good luck)
McCarthy, Joseph (U.S. senator, 1945-1957)
McCarthy Tétrault (legal firm)

M

McClelland & Stewart Ltd. (publisher)
McClelland, Ian (politician)
McClung, Nellie (feminist, 1873-1951)
M'Clure Strait (in Arctic); named after
        explorer Sir Robert M'Clure (1807-73)
McCrae, John (poet, 1872-1918)
McDonald's Restaurants of Canada Ltd.
        –McDonald's
McDonnell Douglas Canada Ltd.
McDonough, Alexa (politician)
McDougall, Barbara (politician)
McGraw-Hill Ryerson Ltd. (publisher)
McIntosh apple
        –*but* Macintosh (computer)
McLachlan, Sarah (singer)
McLaren, Norman (filmmaker, 1914-1987)
McLauchlan, Murray (folksinger)
McLaughlin, Audrey (former NDP leader)
McLuhan, Marshall (1911-1980)
McPherson, Aimee Semple (evangelist, 1890-
        1944)
MDS Inc.
meagre (*not* -ger)
Meals on Wheels
meat packer (*two words*)
Mecca (place)
        –*but* a music mecca
medal, medallist
Medals–Capitalize specific names.
        –Medal of Bravery
        –the Military Medal (MM)
        –a military medal
Medicaid (U.S. program of health care for poor)
medicare (government medical insurance plan
        in general), Medicare (U.S. health program)
medieval
Mediterranean
medium, media (*pl.* — except mediums in spiritualism)
Meech Lake

M

meerschaum (pipe)

mega-city (Toronto)

member

    –member of Parliament (MP, MPs)

    –member of the Order of the British
    Empire (MBE)

    –member of provincial parliament
    (MPP — Ontario only, *but avoid*)

    –member of house of assembly
    (MHA — Nfld. only, *but avoid*)

    –member of legislative assembly
    (MLA, *but avoid*)

    –member of national assembly
    (MNA — Quebec only, *but avoid*)

memento, mementoes

memo, memos

memoir (*not* memoire)

    –*but* aide-mémoire

memorandum, memorandums

Mendelssohn, Felix (composer, 1809-1847)

meningitis, meningococcal disease

Mennonite

menstrual, menstruate

menswear, womenswear

Mercator projection

Mercedes-Benz

merchant marine

Merrill Lynch & Co. Canada Ltd.

Messiah, a messiah

Messrs. — *Use* Messieurs (before names)

meter (gauge); metre (m — *sing.* and *pl.*
    metric symbol, *no period*); *but* diameter

methadone

Métis (mixed Indian and European ancestry)

metre (m — *sing.* and *pl.* metric symbol, *no
    period*); meter (gauge); diameter

metrication (*not* metrification)

Mexico City

MHA (Nfld. only — member of house
of assembly, *but avoid*)
MI-5, MI-6 (British intelligence)
Michigan (Mich.)
mickey (half-sized bottle of liquor)
Micmac (*avoid–use* Mi'kmaq)
micro (*prefix*), microcomputer, microsurgery,
microwave, micro-organism
microphone, mike
midday
Middle Ages
Middle (*not* Near) East
Middle West, Midwest (U.S.)
Mideast
midshipman (*no abbvn.*)
midsummer (*no hyphen*)
midway (*no hyphen*)
MiG (for Russian aircraft designers Mikoyan
and Gurevich)
Mi'kmaq (*not* Micmac)
mileage (*not* milage; for metric, use "consumption" or "fuel consumption")
Military Rank–Plurals add "s" to the
significant rank category, not to the
qualifying word.
–major-generals
–lieutenant-colonels
–sergeants major
–regimental sergeants major
millennium (-nn-), millenniums
Miller, Glenn (band leader, 1904-1944)
Millett, Kate (writer)
millimetre (mm — *sing.* and *pl.* metric
symbol, *no period*)
Milosevic, Slobodan (Serbian leader)
Milquetoast, Caspar
Minamata, Japan
–Minamata disease

M

Mini–Hyphenate unless the non-hyphenated
form is established.
mini-budget, mini-play, mini-restaurant,
mini-series, mini-sub, *but* minibike,
minibus, minicar, minicomputer,
miniskirt, minivan
minimize
minimum, minimums
minister
–Energy Minister Sylvia Carney;
Sylvia Carney, energy minister
Ministry–Capitalize national and provincial
government ministries even when the
full name is not used.
–Ministry of the Interior
–Interior Ministry
–Ministry of Transportation and
Communications
–Communications Ministry
–The freeze affected Industry and Labour.
Minnesota (Minn.)
mint, Royal Canadian Mint, the mint
minus, minuses
minuscule (*not* miniscule)
Minute Rice (trademark for quick-cooking rice)
minutia, minutiae
Miramichi River (N.B.), the Miramichi area
MIRV (for multiple independently targeted
re-entry vehicle; always needs
explanation)
misinterpret, misinterpreter,
misinterpretation
mislead, misled, misleading
Mississauga, Ont.
Mississauga IceDogs
Mississippi (Miss.)
Missouri (Mo.)
Mitchell, Joni (singer)
Mixmaster (trademark for food mixer)

MLA (except Ont., Que. and Nfld. — member
of the legislative assembly) *but avoid*

Mladic, Ratko (Bosnian Serb general)

MNA (Que. — member of national assembly)
but avoid

moccasin

Moffat Communications Ltd.

Mogadishu

Mohammed (founder of Islam, the Muslim religion)
–but Muhammad Ali (Cassius Clay)

Mohawk (*sing.* and *pl.*)

Moldova (formerly Moldavia)

mollusk

Molotov cocktail

Molson Inc.

Moncton Times and Transcript

money, moneys

monitor

monkey, monkeys

Monroe, Marilyn (1926-1962)

monsieur (*no abbvn.*), messieurs

monsignor, Msgr. Ronald Thom
–Thom (or the monsignor) said ...

Montana (Mont.)

Monterey, Calif.

Monterrey (Spain, Mexico)

Montgomery, Lucy Maud (1874-1942)

Months–In dates, abbreviate except March,
April, May, June, July: Jan. 13, 1936;
April 2, 1981, was a Thursday; *but*
January 1999, *no commas.*

moon

Moose Jaw Times-Herald

moral (*n.* — lesson, inner meaning;
adj. — right, just), moralist, morality

morale (*n.* — mental condition, attitude)

Moral Majority (*no* "the")

Morgentaler, Dr. Henry

Morissette, Alanis (singer)

M

Moriyama, Raymond (architect)

morocco leather

Mormons (acceptable in first reference for Church of
 Jesus Christ of Latter-day Saints)

Morrice, J.W. (painter, 1865-1924)

Morse code

Moslem — *See Muslim*

mosquito, mosquitoes

Mother's Day (second Sunday in May)

Mother Teresa

motocross

motorcycle

motto, mottoes

mould (*not* mold)

Mountain–Capitalize when preceding or
 following specific term.
 –Rocky Mountains
 –Mount Edith Cavell (*not* Mt.)

Mountie, Mounties (for RCMP)

Mount Vesuvius

mouse, mousey, mousier

moustache (*not* mus-)

movable (*not* moveable)

Mowat, Farley (author)

MP (member of Parliament), MPs (*pl.*), MP's
 and MPs' (*poss.*)

m.p.h. (miles per hour)

MPP (Ontario only — member of the
 provincial parliament) *but avoid*

MP3.com

MRI (magnetic resonance imaging)

Ms (*no period*)

MuchMusic, MuchMoreMusic

mucous (*adj.* — covered with mucus), mucus
 (*n.* — sticky secretion)

Muhammad Ali

Muise, Mark (politician)

mujahedeen (holy warrior)

mukluk (deerskin boot)

multi-, multicultural, multilateral, multinational,
    multimillionaire, multimillion-dollar, multimedia
mumps (*takes singular verb*)
Murray, Anne (singer)
Muscovite (of Moscow)
muskellunge, muskie
Muslim (*not* Moslem)
Muzak (trademark for recorded background
    music)
MV (motor vessel)
Myanmar (formerly Burma, *n.* and *adj.*)

N

NAACP (National Association for the
      Advancement of Colored People)
naive, naiveté
Namibia (formerly South-West Africa)
Nanaimo Free Press
naphtha
napoleon (French gold coin, pastry)
Naskapi, Naskapis
nation, *but uppercase* as part of
      aboriginal name: Nisga'a Nation
National, The (CBC news program)
National Action Committee on the Status of
      Women (NAC)
National Aeronautics and Space
      Administration (NASA)
national anthem (O Canada)
National Assembly (national legislative body)
      but Quebec national assembly (provincial)
National Citizens' Coalition
National Defence Headquarters (NDHQ, *but avoid*)
National Energy Board (NEB, *but avoid*)
national energy program
National Farmers Union (NFU, *but avoid*)
National Film Board (NFB)
National Gallery, Museum
national government
National Guard (in U.S.)
    –a National Guard unit
    –a national guardsman
National Harbours Board (NHB, *but avoid*)
National Hockey League Players' Association
National Organization for Women (NOW)
National Post, the National Post
National War Memorial (Ottawa)
nationwide (*no hyphen, but prefer* countrywide)
native peoples (includes Indians, Inuit and Métis)
NATO (North Atlantic Treaty Organization)
nautical mile (1.853 kilometres)

N

Navy–Capitalize Royal Canadian Navy when referring
to pre-unification force. For other forces, lowercase
navy when preceded by the name of the country.
  –Royal Canadian Navy until 1968
  –British navy
  –Royal Navy
  –United States navy
  –a navy spokesman
  –U.S. 6th Fleet
  –Home Fleet
  –10th Destroyer Flotilla
Nazi (party supporter)
Nazism
NBC (National Broadcasting Co.)
  –NBC is acceptable in all references.
N'djamena (Chad)
Nebraska (Neb.)
Negro, Negroes (*use* black)
neighbour, neighbourhood
Neilson Ltd., William (confectioner)
Neo-Confucianism
nerve-racking
Netanyahu, Benjamin
Netherlands, the
  –UTRECHT, Netherlands (placeline)
Nevada (Nev.)
New Brunswick Telegraph-Journal
new Canadian
New China news agency (Xinhua)
New Democratic Party (NDP)
New England
newfangled (*one word*)
New Hampshire (N.H.)
New Jersey (N.J.)
newlyweds
New Mexico (N.M.)
news, newsdesk, newsman, newspaperman,
  newspaperwoman, newsprint,
  newsroom, newsstand

Newspaper Guild, the; the guild

Newspaper Names–Lowercase *the* in names
of newspapers: the Toronto Star; the
Star; the New York Times, the Times. For
French-language papers, write Montreal
La Presse rather than the Montreal La
Presse in first reference. In subsequent
references avoid sentence constructions
that juxtapose *the* and *le* and *la*: the La
Presse editorial. Alternatives include La
Presse said in an editorial, an editorial in
La Presse.

Newsworld (CBC)

New Testament

New Westminster, B.C.

New World

New Year's Eve, New Year's Day *but* the
new year (*lowercase*)

New York (N.Y.)
–New York City
–New York Thruway

Niagara Escarpment, Peninsula

Niagara-on-the-Lake, Ont.

Nichol, bp (poet, 1944-1988)

nickel (coin or metal)

Nicknames–Capitalize nicknames generally.
–the Old Man
–Reds (for Communists)
–the Queen City (Regina)
–the City (London financial area)
–Iron Curtain
–Dave (Tiger) Williams (brackets, not quotes)

niece

Nielsen, A. C. (market researcher), Nielsen ratings

night, guest night, ladies night

nightcap, nightclub, nightdress, nightgown,
nighthawk, night letter, nightlight,
nightmare, night owl, night school,
nightshirt, nighttime, night watch

N

Nike

Nikon (camera)

Nineteen Eighty-Four (George Orwell novel
    but 1984 for Michael Radford movie)

Nisga'a, Nisga'a Nation

nitroglycerine

no, noes
    –but She voted No in the referendum.

Nobel Prize, Nobel Prizes
    –Nobel Peace Prize
    –Nobel Prize in chemistry, physics, etc. but
    Nobel chemistry prize
    –Nobel Memorial Prize in Economic
    Science
    –Nobel Prize winner, laureate
    –Nobel Prize-winning researcher
    –the prize (*lowercase*)

no man's land

nom de plume, noms de plume

noncommittal

nondescript

non-existent (*not* -ant)

nonplus (*v.*), nonplussed

no one (*two words*)

Norad (North American Aerospace Defence Command)

Nortel Networks Corp.

North–Capitalize regions but not their
    derivatives. Lowercase mere direction or
    position.
    –the North (region of Canada)
    –a northerner
    –the northern territories
    –northern natives
    –Northern Canada
    –the Canadian North
    –northern Ontario, northern Quebec, etc.
    –the Far North
    –the North Slope (Alaska)
    –north of the border

–North-South dialogue
–the northern delegation
–the northern states
–The North defeated the South.
–North Atlantic
–Northern Ireland

North American Aerospace Defence
    Command (Norad)
North American Free Trade Agreement (NAFTA)
North Atlantic Treaty Organization (NATO)
North Carolina (N.C.)
North Dakota (N.D.)
northeast, northwest (*one word*)
Northern Hemisphere
northern lights
northern Ontario
northern states (of U.S.)
North Pole, the Pole
North Sea
North Vietnam
Northwest Atlantic Fisheries Organization
    (*no abbvn.*)
North West Company
North West Mounted Police
Northwest Passage
Northwest Rebellion (1885)
Northwest Territories (*but* N.W.T.)
    –Northwest Territories council
nose, nosy, nosier
nostalgia, nostalgic
Notre-Dame Basilica (Montreal)
Nouvelles Télé-Radio (NTR, the French-
    language service of Broadcast News)
Nouvelliste, Le (newspaper in Trois Rivières, Que.)
Nova Corp. (*not* NOVA Corporation of Alberta)
Nova Scotia Power Corp. (*no abbvn.*)
Novocain (trademark for a local anesthetic)
NOW (National Organization for Women)
'N Sync (musical group)

NTR (Nouvelles Télé-Radio)
nucleus, nuclei
number, number 2, No. 2
numskull (*not* numbskull)
Nunassiaq, N.W.T.
Nunavut (Canadian territory)
Nunavummiut (resident of Nunavut)
Nunziata, John (politician)
Nuremberg, Germany
Nureyev, Rudolf (ballet, 1938-1993)
nylon
Nystrom, Lorne (politician)

Oakland Athletics, Oakland A's
O&Y Properties Corp. (*no periods, no spaces* in O&Y)
oasis, oases
Oath of Allegiance (Canada's official oath)
obbligato
Oberammergau
Obhrai, Deepak (politician)
objet d'art, objets d'art
O Canada
occasion
Occidental (race; *but avoid*)
occur, occurred, occurrence, occurring
Ocean–Capitalize with specific name.
  –Pacific Ocean
  –the Atlantic and Pacific oceans
  –an ocean wave
October Crisis (1970)
octopus, octopuses
Odd Fellows, Independent Order of (IOOF,
  but avoid), an Odd Fellow
Odesa, Ukraine (*not* Odessa)
odour, odourless *but* odorous
OECD (Organization for Economic
  Co-operation and Development)
Oedipus
off, offbeat, off-centre, off-duty, off-line,
  off-season, offshore, offside, offstage,
  off-white; blastoff (*n.*), blast off (*v.*).
  Similarly: cutoff, layoff, payoff, playoff, sendoff,
  standoff, stopoff, takeoff (all *n.*)
offence, offensive
office, county clerk's office
  –Home Office (U.K.)
  –Foreign Office (U.K.)
officer cadet (*no abbvn.*)
  –Officer Cadet John Sampson
officer of the Order of the British Empire (OBE)
officers mess
Oh! Calcutta! (revue)

O

Ohio (*no abbvn.*)

oilfield, oilpatch, oilsands (*one word*)

Ojibwa (Indian — rhymes with way) (*sing.* and *pl.*)

OK (*not* okay), OK'd, OK'ing

Oklahoma (Okla.)

Oklahoma! (musical)

Oktoberfest (beer-drinking festival)

old age pension

Old Boys network

old-fashioned

Old Testament

old-time, old-timer

Olivier, Laurence (1907-1989)

Olympic Games, the Games
      —the Winter Olympics, the Olympics,
      the Summer Games

ombudsman, ombudsmen
      —ombudsman Jill Leonard

omelette

Onassis, Aristotle (1906-1975)

Ondaatje, Michael

One-Eleven (British aircraft)

onetime (*adj.*, *one word*; former: a onetime actor)
      —one-time (*adj.*, *hyphen*; once only: a
      one-time payment)

online (all uses)

onstage, offstage

Ontarian

Ontario Health Insurance Plan (OHIP, *but avoid*)

Ontario Provincial Police (*but* the provincial police)

on to
      —*but* He drove onto the beach.

ONtv (Ontario network)

OPEC (Organization of Petroleum Exporting Countries)

openness

ophthalmologist, ophthalmology

Opposition—Capitalize when referring to the
      official Opposition. Otherwise, lowercase.
      —an opposition viewpoint, sat in opposition

–the Opposition leader

oppress, oppression, oppressive

opus, opuses

Orange Crush (trademark for pop)

orbit (*n.* and *v.*), orbital, orbiting

Order of Canada

—companion of the Order of Canada
(recipients may use initials CC)

—officer of the order (initials OC)

—member of the order (initials CM)

order-in-council, orders-in-council

ordinary seaman (*no abbvn.*)

—Ordinary Seaman Alain Delisle

Oregon (Ore.)

Organization for Economic Co-operation and
Development (OECD)

Organization of African Unity (OAU)

Organization of American States (OAS)

Organization of Petroleum Exporting
Countries (OPEC)

organize

Orient, Oriental (race; *but use* Asia, Asian)

—an oriental flavour

—Orient Express (train)

Orillia Packet and Times

Orlon (trademark for acrylic fabric)

orneriness, ornery

ornithology

orthopedic

Osgoode Hall (home of Ontario Supreme Court)

Otello (Verdi and Rossini operas), Othello
(Shakespeare play)

Ottawa Rough Riders (*but* Saskatchewan
Roughriders)

Ottawa 67's (hockey team)

Ouellet, André

out, outbid, outboard, outbox, outfield,
outpatient, *but* out-take (film);
fadeout (*n.*), fade out (*v.*). Similarly:

O

fallout, hideout, pullout, shootout,
shutout, takeout, walkout (all *n.*)
Outaouais, western Quebec
Oval Office
overall, overalls (garment)
overall (all-embracing)
Owen Sound Sun Times
Oxfam-Canada
oxford (cloth, shoe)
Ozawa, Seiji (conductor)
ozone

Pablum (trademark for a baby cereal),
    but pabulum (food)
pact, Baghdad Pact, Warsaw Pact
page 2, pages 1-3; p. 2, pp. 1-3 (*abbvn.* for tabulation)
Pahlavi, Mohammad Reza (shah, 1919-1980)
paleontologist, paleontology
Palestine Liberation Organization (PLO)
pallbearer (*one word*)
panacea
Panama Canal
panama hat
Panama, Isthmus of
Pan American Games, Pan Am Games (*no hyphen*)
PanCanadian Petroleum Ltd.
panda (*not* panda bear)
panel, panellist, panelling
Pankiw, Jim (politician)
panorama
pantsuit
pantyhose
paparazzo, paparazzi
paper, paperback, paperbacked, paperbound,
    paper-boy, paper-clip, paper-girl,
    paperhanger, paperweight, paperwork
Pap smear, test
Papua New Guinea (*no hyphen*)
paraffin (wax; in Britain, kerosene)
paragraph 2
parallel, paralleled, 49th parallel
paralyse (*not* -ze), paralysis
paranoia, paranoiac, paranoid
paraphernalia (*pl.*)
paraplegic
parenthesis, parentheses
parimutuel (*no hyphen*)
Parisien Libéré (newspaper — *not* Libre)
park, Banff National Park, High Park
Parkinson's disease, Parkinsonism

P

parliament
 –Parliament (national legislature)
 –parliament (provincial or regional)
 –parliamentary
 –Parliament Buildings (Ottawa)
Parliament, member of (MP, MPs)
parlour
Parmesan cheese
parole, paroled, parolee
Parti indépendantiste
Parti Québécois (PQ), Québécois's (*poss.*)
 –Péquiste (*n., adj.*)
partisan
part time, a part-time job, a part-timer
party, Communist party, Green party,
  Liberal party
 –*but* New Democratic Party (NDP)
 –Parti Québécois (PQ)
Passchendaele
passerby, passersby
pasteurize, pasteurizing (*lowercase*)
pastime
patchwork (*one word*)
pavilion (*not* pavillion)
Pavarotti, Luciano
paycheque (*one word*)
pay day (*two words*)
pay off (*v.*), payoff (*n.*)
payola
payroll (*no hyphen*)
pay TV, pay TV network (*no hyphen*)
PCB (polychlorinated biphenyl), PCBs
pea, peameal bacon, pea soup, pea-soup
  fog, pea-souper (fog)
Peace Corps (U.S.)
peacekeeping
peacemaker
peacetime
peak (mountain, apex); peek (peer)

peccadillo, peccadillos
pedagogy
pedal (bicycle), pedaller, pedalling
peddle (to sell), pedlar (seller), peddling,
softpedal (*not* -peddle)
pediatrician
pedlar (seller)
pedophile
peewee
Peggy's Cove, N.S.
pekinese (dog)
pemmican (dried meat)
Penetanguishene, Ont.
penicillin
penitentiary, Kingston Penitentiary
Pennsylvania (Pa.)
pension, Canada Pension Plan (CPP, *but avoid*)
Pepsi, Pepsi-Cola (trademarks for a cola drink)
pep talk (*two words*)
Péquiste
perceive, perceived, perceiving
per cent, percentage, six per cent increase (*no hyphens*)
perennial
perestroika
perfunctory
periphery
permafrost (*no hyphen*)
permissible (*not* -able)
perogy, perogies
perquisite (perk), prerequisite (requirement)
Perrier (trademark for a mineral water)
perseverance, persevere, persevering
Pershing, Pershing 2 missile
Persian Gulf War
persian lamb
persistence (*not* -ance), persistency,
persistent (*not* -ant)
persona non grata
persuade, persuadable, persuasible,

P

persuasion, persuasive
Petro-Canada (*hyphen; no abbvn. except in texts*)
petrochemical (*no hyphen*)
petty officer (*no abbvn.*)
   –chief petty officer (first class) (*no abbvn.*)
   –petty officer (first class) (*no abbvn.*)
PGA (Professional Golfers Association)
Phalange party (Lebanon)
pharaoh
phase, Phase 1 (*not* phase one)
PhD (doctor of philosophy)
phenomenon, phenomena
Philadelphia Inquirer (newspaper)
Philadelphia 76ers (*no apostrophe*)
Philip (usual spelling of first name)
   –Prince Philip
Philippe
Philippines, the
   –QUEZON CITY, Philippines (placeline)
   –Filipinos (the people)
Philistine (*one* l)
Phnom Penh, Cambodia
Phoebe
phone (*no apostrophe*)
phoney (*not* phony), phoneys
phosphorus (*not* -ous)
photocopy (*n. and v.*), photocopier (*n.*)
photo-engraver, photo-engraving
piastre (*not* -er)
piccolo, piccolos
picket (*not* picketer), picketed, picketing
pick up (*v.*), pickup (*n. or adj.*)
picnic, picnicker
piecemeal
pigeonhole (*no hyphen*)
pill (lowercase for birth control pill; use a
   descriptive phrase if necessary)
pilot officer (*no abbvn.*)
pinch-hitter

Pinot Noir, Blanc (wine)
pin up (*v.*), pin-up (*n.*)
pipeline
     –*but* TransCanada PipeLines Ltd.
pizzazz
placeline
     –CORNER BROOK, Nfld.
     –MacGREGOR, Man. (for MacGregor)
     –MACKENZIE, B.C. (for Mackenzie)
Placer Dome Inc.
Places–*See Locations*
plagiarism, plagiarize
plainclothes police
     –police in plain clothes
plan, Colombo Plan, Marshall Plan
     but the Hungarian five-year plan
plaster of paris
plateau, plateaus
platoon sergeant (Platoon Sgt.)
platypus, platypuses
play off (*v.*), playoff (*n.*)
playwright, *but* playwriting
PLC (public limited company)
Plexiglas (trademark for an acrylic plastic)
PLO (Palestine Liberation Organization)
plow (*not* plough)
plummet, plummeted
plus, pluses
p.m., a.m.
pogey (slang for unemployment insurance)
poinsettia
Point Lepreau
Polanyi, John (Nobel Prize in chemistry, 1986)
Polaroid (trademark for camera, sunglasses)
Pole, the; North Pole, South Pole
Police–Uppercase when using the formal
     name of a force. Otherwise, lowercase.
     –provincial police, regional police
     –Toronto Police Service, *but* a Toronto police

officer, Toronto police
–Ontario Provincial Police (OPP)
–*but* Quebec provincial police (*no abbvn.*)
–Royal Canadian Mounted Police (RCMP)
–Mounties (for RCMP)
–police chief
–police Chief Arnold Goldberg
–police commission
–Quebec police commission
_police court, station

policy-maker

polio (short for poliomyelitis)

Politburo

Politics–Capitalize political parties, as Liberal, Labour, Socialist, *but* lowercase the words when referring to philosophical attitudes. Capitalize Opposition when referring to the official Opposition, the non-governing party with most seats.

polka-dot (*hyphen*)

Pollyanna

Ponteix, Sask.

pontiff (for Pope)

pope, Pope John Paul, the Pope (current pontiff), former pope, popes of history

Popsicle (trademark for ice on a stick)

pore (*v.* — study earnestly), pored, poring

Porsche

Portage la Prairie, Man.

Port aux Basques, Nfld.

porterhouse steak

portland cement

Portuguese

postdate (*v.*), postdated cheque

postelection

post-game

postgraduate

postmaster general, postmasters general

post-mortem (*hyphen*)

P

post-season (*hyphen*)
post-secondary
postwar
potato, potatoes
potlatch (aboriginal gift, ceremony)
potshot
PoW (prisoner of war), PoWs
power of attorney (*no hyphens*)
powwow (*n.* and *v.*)
PR (for public relations)
practicable (can be done), practical (useful, functional)
practice (*n.* or *adj.*), practise (*v.*)
prairie
    –Prairie provinces
    –the Prairies
    –the prairie stretched for miles
    –their Prairie farm
pre, prearrange, Precambrian shield,
    pre-Christian, precondition, predate,
    pre-election, pre-empt, preheat,
    premarital, preoccupy, prepaid,
    preschool, preschooler, pre-season, pretax,
    prewar
precede, precedence (priority)
precedent (earlier instance)
prefer, preferable, preferably, preference (*not*
    -ance), preferential, preferred
Premier–Use for Canadian provinces,
    Australian states, France and former
    French colonies.
    –Premier Ann Bostwick
    –deputy premier Henry Miller
    –premiers conference
    –former premier Roy Romanow
    –the premier of Ontario
première (*n.* and *v.*)
    –*but* a premier attraction
prerequisite (requirement), perquisite (perk)
prerogative (*not* perog-)

P

Presbyterian Church in Canada
president, President Bill Clinton
> –the president said ...
> –former president Bill Clinton
> –president-elect Ronald Reagan
> –GM president John Brown

Presque Isle, Me.
Presqu'ile Point, Ont.
press gallery
> –Parliamentary Press Gallery Association
> –press gallery dinner
> –worked in the press gallery

Presse, La (Montreal newspaper)
Presse Canadienne, La (PC)
pre-tax (*hyphen*)
pretence
prevalence, prevalent
prevent, preventable, preventer (*not* -or),
> preventive (*not* preventative)

price tag (*two words*)
pricey
Primakov, Yevgeny (Russia)
Prime minister–Use for national government
> leaders except when premier or other
> titles – German chancellor – are conventional.
> *See premier*
> –Prime Minister Ellen McKay
> –the prime minister said ...
> –the Prime Minister's Office (PMO)
> –former prime minister Ellen McKay
> –prime minister-designate Ellen McKay
> –Deputy Prime Minister Ellen McKay

prime time, prime-time program
prince
> –Prince Charles, Charles, the prince;
> Charles, Prince of Wales; the Prince of Wales

Prince Edward Island, the Island
princess
> –Princess Anne, Anne, the princess

–but the Princess of Wales or Diana (*not* Princess Diana)

Princess Patricia's Canadian Light Infantry

principal (main, most important), school principal
  –school principal Paul Chambers

principle (fundamental belief)

prison, Oakalla prison farm

prisoner of war (PoW, PoWs)

private (Pte. Bob Lively)
  –private first class (Pte. 1st Class)

privatize, privatization

privilege

Privy Council (*uppercase*)
  –Privy Council Office (*no abbvn.*)

processor, word processor

Procter and Gamble Inc.

prodigy, prodigies, prodigious

professor, Prof. Normand Saint-Onge

program (*not* -mme), programmer, programming
  –national energy program

Prohibition (alcohol outlawed)

Promised Land

promulgate, promulgation, promulgator (*not* -er)

proofread

propaganda

propellant (*n.*), propellent (*adj.*)

propeller (*not* -or)

prophecy (*n.*), prophesy (*v.*)

prorogue

prospectus, prospectuses

prostate (male gland); prostrate (lying face down; overcome)

Protestant, Protestantism (religion)

protester (*not* -or)

province, provincial
  –province of Ontario (geog.)
  –Province of Ontario bonds (corp.)

provincewide

P

proviso, provisos
Prud'homme, Marcel (senator)
p's and q's
psychedelic
psychiatric, psychiatrist, psychiatry
psychic
psychopath, psychopathic
psychosis, psychoses
psychosomatic
public, public library
    –public school board
    –public utilities commission
publicly (*never* publically)
Pulitzer Prize
    –a Pulitzer Prize-winning writer
pulley, pulleys
pulp mill (*two words*)
Punxsutawney, Pa.
Pushkin, Alexander
push over (*v.*), pushover (*n.*)
push up (*v.*), pushup (*n.*)
Putin, Vladimir
putt (golf)
Pygmy
pyjamas
Pyrex (trademark for heat-resistant cookware)

Qantas Airways
Qatar
Q-Tips (trademark for cotton swabs on a stick)
quadriplegic
Quai d'Orsay (French Foreign Ministry)
Quakers (Society of Friends)
quandary
Qu'Appelle, Sask.
quarter-final *but* semifinal
quarter-horse
quartet
quarto, quartos
Quebec City (*but* Quebec in placelines)
Quebecer (*not* -ck)
Québécois, Parti Québécois (PQ)
Quebecor Inc.
Quebec provincial police (*lowercase, no abbvn.*)
Queen (of Canada), queen (other nations)
Queen Elizabeth 2 (liner), QE2
Queen Mother
Queen's counsel (QC)
Queen's Park
Queen's Plate
Queen's University, Kingston, Ont.
questionnaire
question period (*lowercase*)
quiche Lorraine
Quotidien, Le (newspaper in Chicoutimi, Que.)
quixotic (extravagantly chivalrous; from Don Quixote)
Qur'an (*not* Koran)

rabbi, Rabbi Stuart E. Rosenberg

raccoon, raccoons

race, race card, racecourse, race horse,
    racetrack, raceway

racked (their brains)

racket (bat used in tennis, badminton, etc.)

racquetball (game)

radioactive

Radio-Canada (*hyphen*)

Radio Moscow (*but* Moscow radio)

Radio, Television Stations–Use this style:
    CFCF Montreal, CHUM-FM Toronto,
    CBC-TV

radius, radii

railway (*preferred to* railroad)
    –*but* Long Island Rail Road

railworker

rain, raindrop, rainfall, rainforest, rainstorm

RAM (random access memory)

Ramadan

rancour *but* rancorous

R and B (rhythm and blues)

R and D (research and development)

R and R (rest and recreation)

Ranger 4 (satellite)

rapt (absorbed, intent)

rarefy, rarefied

rational (sensible)

rationale (statement of reasons)

raucous (*not* -cus)

rayon

razzmatazz (*no hyphens*)

re-, readmit, reassess, recur, recurrence,
    re-examine, re-enter, reinstate, reissue,
    reopen, reorganize, re-cover (cover
    again), recover (regain), re-lay (lay again),
    relay (pass on), reroute, rerun, re-sign
    (sign again), resign (quit), reunite, reuse,
    reusable

R

Reader's Digest (*not* Readers')

ready-made (*hyphen*)

reality, realization, realize (*not* -ise)

Realtor–In Canada, a trademark and must be capitalized. Not a synonym for real estate agent. It identifies members of the Canadian Real Estate Association and the (U.S.) National Association of Realtors: agents or brokers, *but* also property managers, developers and other real estate professionals.

REAL Women

rearguard

Rebagliati, Ross (Olympic medallist)

rebut, refute (prove wrong; *use with care*)

recoilless

recommend

Red (Communist, *but avoid*)

Red Cross, Red Cross Society, Red Crescent
–a Red Cross campaign

redneck (rustic, poor white)

Reeves, Keanu

refer, referred

referendum, referendums

Reformation (event)

reformatory, Guelph reformatory

refuel, refuelled

refute, rebut (prove wrong; *use with care*)

reggae

regiment, 24th Regiment

regimental sergeant major (Regimental Sgt. Maj.)
–regimental sergeants major (*no abbvn.*)

Regina Leader-Post

registered retirement savings plan (RRSP)

reign (rule), rein (leather strap, symbol of power)

Religion–Capitalize names of religions and denominations.
–American Lutheran Church
–Anglican Church of Canada

R

 -Baha'i faith
 -Buddhism, Buddhist
 -Church of Jesus Christ of Latter-day Saints
 -Greek Orthodox Church
 -Islam
 -Jehovah's Witnesses
 -Judaism (Orthodox, Reform, Conservative)
 -Pentecostal Assembly
 -Presbyterian Church in Canada
 -Roman Catholic Church
 -Seventh-day Adventist
 -Ukrainian Orthodox Church
 -United Church of Canada

relinquish

R.E.M. (musical group)

Remembrance Day (Nov. 11)

reminiscent

removable (*not* -eable)

remuneration

Renaissance (historic period), a renaissance of
 painting (general sense)

renowned

repechage (rowing)

repel, repellent

repent, repentance, repentant

repertoire, repertory

repetition, repetitious

representative
 -Representative Chris Flynn (D — Mass.)
 -Representative Robert Brown (R — Calif.)

reprieve

republic, Fifth Republic
 -Republic of Ireland
 -the Irish republic

republican (philosophical attitude)

Republican (party or member)
 -Senator John Smith (R — Calif.)
 -Representative Mary Brown (R — Ohio)
 -Republican party (U.S.)

R

requiem, requiem mass

research and development, R and D (*no periods*)

reserve (*preferred to* reservation for aboriginal lands), the Chippewa reserve

re-sign (sign again), resign (quit)

resistance, resistibility, resistible (*not* -able)

respectability, respectable

restaurateur (*not* restauranteur)

resumé

resuscitate

retired, retired brigadier Pat Turner

retro-rocket (*hyphen*)

Reuters (all uses)
    –Reuters news agency, (Reuters)

reverend
    –Rev. Alan Cross — (Protestant and RC; Cross *on second reference*)

reverse, reversible

revolution, American Revolution

revolutions per minute (r.p.m.)

Reye's syndrome

Rh (for Rhesus) factor, Rh positive, Rh negative

rhinoceros (*sing.* and *pl.*)

Rhode Island (R.I.)

Rhodes Scholar, Scholarship

rhododendron

Richler, Mordecai (author)

Richter scale

Richthofen, Baron von (Red Baron, 1892-1918)

ricochet, ricocheted

Rideau Hall

rifleman (*no abbvn.*)
    –Rifleman Andrew Coates

right, right field, right-fielder, right wing, right-winger; right-field wall, right-handed pitcher, right-wing politician (*adj., hyphen*)

right-handed, right-hander (*hyphen*)

rigor mortis
rigour *but* rigorous
Riis, Nelson (politician)
Rio Algom Ltd.
Rio de Janeiro
rip off (*v.*), ripoff (*n.*)
river, St. Lawrence River
Riyadh
RJR-Macdonald Inc.
Road–Capitalize when used with names,
      abbreviate in numbered street addresses.
      –along Kingston Road
      –10 Scott Rd. E.
roadblock (*one word*)
Robinson, Svend (politician)
ROBTv (specialty channel)
Rock, Allan (politician)
Rock, the (informal for Newfoundland or Gibraltar)
Rockefeller Centre
rock 'n' roll
rococo
Rodrigue (given name — *not* -que)
Rogers Communications Inc.
rollcall (*one word*)
Rollerblades (trademark for in-line skates),
Rollerblading (*but use* in-line skating)
roller-coaster, roller derby, roller-skate (*v.*),
      roller skates
rollover (*n.*)
Rolls-Royce Ltd., a Rolls-Royce
roly-poly (*hyphen*)
ROM (read only memory)
Roman Catholic (Roman may be dropped only if
     reference is obvious)
Romanesque
Romania (*not* Rumania)
Roman Numerals–Use roman numerals to
     indicate sequence for people and animals
     and in proper names where specified.

Otherwise prefer arabic numerals as
easier to grasp.
–Pope Pius XII, Henry VIII,
The Godfather, Part II

roman numerals, type
roof, roofs
room, Room 4, Oak Room
       –in the assembly room
Rorschach test
Rosh Hashanah
Rothmans Inc.
Rothschild
Rotisserie League Baseball (trademark for fantasy
       baseball league)
Rough Riders, Ottawa (*but* Saskatchewan Roughriders)
roundup (*n.*), round up (*v.*)
Royal Air Force
royal assent
Royal Bank of Canada
Royal Canadian Air Force until 1968
Royal Canadian Legion
       –the legion announced ...
       –parade of legionnaires
Royal Canadian Mounted Police (RCMP)
       –RCMP musical ride
       –the Mounties
Royal Canadian Navy until 1968
royal commission — *See commission*
Royal Family (British), royal family (other
       nations)
Royal Ontario Museum (ROM, *but avoid*)
royal tour, visit
royalty
r.p.m. (revolutions per minute)
RRSP (registered retirement savings plan)
ruble
rumour
runner-up, runners-up
run-off

rural route
        –RR 2, Newmarket
rush hour, rush-hour traffic
Russia
Rwanda
RV (for recreational vehicle)
Ryerson Polytechnic University (Toronto)

'S – To denote the possessive add 's to singular and
plural nouns not ending in "s": mother's purse,
women's shoes, alumni's gifts. Add it to singular nouns
ending in "s" to indicate a sis or siz sound: the boss's
secretary, Strauss's waltzes, Duplessis's cabinet. But if
adding an s would make the word hard to say, add an
apostrophe alone: Ann Landers' column, Richard
Rodgers' music, Jesus' disciples.

saccharin (*n.*), saccharine (*adj.*)

sacrilegious

Sadler's Wells Ballet

Sailboats–Capitalize names of classes of
racing and pleasure craft.
–Tornado, International Europe

St-, Ste-, St.–Use abbreviations in federal
and provincial names of political ridings.

St. Bernard (dog)

St. Catharines, Ont.

St. Catharines Standard

Ste-Catherine Street (Montreal)

St-Hilaire, Caroline (politician)

St-Hyacinthe

St-Jacques, Diane (politician)

St-Jean-Baptiste Day (June 24, also Fête nationale)

St-Jean, Que.

Saint John, N.B.

Saint John Times-Globe

St. John Ambulance

St. John of Jerusalem, Most Venerable Order
of the Hospital of (usually Order of St. John)

St. John River (N.B.)

St. John's, Nfld.

Saint-Laurent, Louis

St. Lawrence Seaway, the seaway
–St. Lawrence Seaway Authority
–St. Lawrence Seaway Development
Corp. (U.S.)

St. Marguerite Bourgeoys (Canada's first
woman saint, 1620-1700)

S

St. Martin-in-the-Fields, Academy of, Church
Saint Mary's University (Halifax)
St. Marys, Ont.
Sainte-Marie, Buffy (singer-composer)
St. Petersburg (formerly Leningrad)
St-Pierre-Miquelon (islands)
  –St-Pierre (capital city)
St. Thomas Times-Journal
St. Valentine's Day, Valentine's Day (Feb. 14)
  –*but* a valentine (card)
salability, salable (*not* -eable)
Salchow, triple Salchow (figure-skating jump)
salmonella
SALT (for strategic arms limitation talks)
Salvadoran
Salvation Army, the Army, a Salvationist
salvo, salvos (*pl.*)
SAM (for surface-to-air missile)
Samaritan, Good
Sanaa, Yemen
sanatorium, sanatoriums
sanctimonious
Sanforized (trademark)
San Francisco 49ers (*no apostrophe*)
Sanka (trademark for a decaffeinated coffee)
sapper (*no abbvn.*)
  –Sapper John Flynn
Sarajevo
Saran Wrap (trademark for a plastic film)
Saskatchewan (*not* Regina) Roughriders (*one
  word — but* Ottawa Rough Riders)
Saskatchewan Party
saskatoon (berry)
Saskatoon StarPhoenix
sasquatch (mysterious ape-like creature)
Satan, satanic, Satanism
satellite — *See Space*
Sault Ste. Marie, Ont. and Mich.
  –the Sault (*not* the Soo)

–but Soo Greyhounds hockey team
Sauvageau, Benoit (politician)
Savile Row (London)
saviour, Saviour (Christ)
savory (herb)
savour, savoury (flavour)
saxophone
Scandinavia
scare, scary, scarier
scarf, scarves
scarlet fever
Scene 2, the second scene
sceptic — *Use* skeptic
Schafer, R. Murray (composer)
Schefferville, Que.
schizophrenia, schizophrenic
scholar, Rhodes Scholar, Scholarship
school, elementary and high
    –day school, private school
    –Leaside high school
    –Sunday school
    –St. Mary's school (elementary or high)
    –School of Practical Science (*no abbvn.*)
    –the McGill medical school
    –London School of Economics
    –University of Toronto Schools
    –Vancouver school board
    school board, schoolbook, schoolboy,
    school bus, schoolgirl, school guard,
    schoolmarm, school teacher,
    school trustee, schoolyard
Schumann, Robert (composer, 1810-1856)
Schwarzenegger, Arnold
Scotch Tape (trademark for sticky tape)
scotch whisky
Scots or Scottish (*not* Scotch)
Scotsman (*not* Scotchman)
scout
    –Scouts Canada

–the Scouts (association)
–a scout
–eagle scout (U.S.)
–Beaver
–Cub
–Chief Scout's Award
–Venturer Scout, Venturers

Scrabble (trademark for a word game)

Screech (rum)

Scripture (Bible)

S-curve

scuttlebutt (*no hyphen*)

Sea–Capitalize when preceding or following the specific term.
  –Sea of Galilee
  –Black Sea

Sea-Doo (trademark for a brand of personal watercraft)

Seafarers' International Union (SIU)

seaman
  –able seaman (*no abbvn.*)
  –leading seaman (*no abbvn.*)
  –ordinary seaman (*no abbvn.*)

Sears Canada Inc.
  –a Sears store, Sears

Seasons–Lowercase for spring, summer, fall
  or autumn, winter

season's greetings

seat-belt (*hyphen*)

SEATO (for Southeast Asia Treaty Organization)

seaway, St. Lawrence Seaway
  –St. Lawrence Seaway Authority
  –St. Lawrence Seaway Development Corp.

second lieutenant (2nd Lieut. Marie Demers)

Second World War (*not* World War II)

secretary general (*no hyphen*)

Section 23, Sec. 5

Security Council (UN)

Seeing Eye (trademark for guide dog)

seigneur, seigniory

semi, semi-annual, semicircle, semicolon,
  semifinal (*but* quarter-final), semifinalist,

S

semi-invalid, semi-official, semitransparent,
semitropical, semi-weekly
Semite, Semitism, anti-Semitism
Senate (national legislature)
–the university senate
senator (*no abbvn.*)
–Senator Barbara Jensen (PC — Manitoba)
–Senator John McLean (D — Mass.)
–former senator Robert de Cotret
senior chief petty officer (*no abbvn.*)
sensual (gratifying to the body, especially
sexually), sensuous (appealing to the
senses, especially through beauty)
separate school, school board
Serb (*n.*), Serbian (*adj.*)
sergeant (Sgt. Margaret Bonotto)
–staff sergeant (Staff Sgt. Margaret Bonotto)
sergeant-at-arms
sergeant first class (Sgt. 1st Class)
sergeant major (Sgt. Maj. Fred Tylee)
–regimental sergeant major (Regimental Sgt. Maj.)
–sergeants major (*pl.*)
series (*generally lowercase*)
–*but* World Series, the Series, Little
League World Series
set up (*v.*), setup (*n.*)
Seventh-day Adventist
Seven-Up Canada Inc.
–Seven-Up Toronto
–Seven-Up Montréal ltée (*no period*)
–7Up (soft drink)
sewage (waste), sewerage (drainage)
Sex and the City (TV show, *not* Sex in the City)
sextet
shakable (*not* -eable)
shake down (*v.*), shakedown (*n.* and *adj.*)
Shakespeare, Shakespearean
shake up (*v.*), shakeup (*n.*)
shaky, shakier, shakiness

S

shalom (greeting)
shaman, shamans (*pl.*), Shamanism
shanghai (*v.*), shanghaied, shanghaiing
Shangri-La
shanty, shanties
Sharansky, Natan
Shaw Communications Inc.
sheik (*not* shiek)
shellac, shellacking
shemozzle (commotion)
sheriff, Sheriff Anton Gerber
Sheshatshiu, Labrador (formerly Sheshatsheit)
Shiite Muslim
Shippagan, N.B. (*not* Shippegan)
shipwreck (*no hyphen*)
Shirleys Bay, Ont. (*no apostrophe*)
shish kebab
shivaree (friendly invasion of newlyweds' home)
shlemiel (foolish, unlucky person)
shlep (to drag)
shlock (shoddy)
shmaltz (sentimentality)
shmo (a fool, a clumsy person)
shmooz (chat)
shnook (a patsy)
shnorrer (a moocher, panhandler)
shoo-in
shoot out (*v.*), shootout (*n.*)
short list (*n.*) shortlist (*v.*)
shortwave (broadcasting)
shotgun (*one word*)
shot put (*two words*)
show, flower show, horse show
shtick (a gimmick; clowning)
shut out (*v.*), shutout (*n.*)
siamese twins (*prefer* joined twins or description:
        babies born attached at the hips)
side-effect
Sidney, B.C.

siege (*not* -ei-)
sight, sightseeing, sightseer
signal, signalled, signaller
signalman (no abbvn.)
      –Signalman William O'Callaghan
Sikh, the Sikh religion
Siksika (aboriginal band)
silhouette
Silicon Valley
silo, silos
Simoniz (trademark for a car wax)
Sinn Fein
sinus, sinuses
siphon (*not* syphon)
sir, Sir John Jones; Sir John *or preferably*
      Jones in second reference
sirocco (Italian name for Sahara wind)
sitcom (TV situation comedy)
Sites–*See Locations*
sizable (*not* -eable)
skating, figure skating, ice skating, speed
      skating (*hyphenate when used adjectivally*)
skeptic, skeptical, skepticism (*not* sc-)
ski, skier, skis, skiing
Ski-Doo (snowmobile trademark)
skid row (*not* road)
skilful
skulduggery
SkyDome
slaughterhouse
slew (large number — *but avoid*)
smallmouth (bass)
Smallwood, Joey (*not* Joseph, 1900-1991)
smart-alec
Smiths Falls, Ont. (*no apostrophe*)
Smithsonian Institution (*not* Institute)
smoky (*not* smokey)
smorgasbord
smoulder

S

snakehead (human smuggler)

sneaked (*not* snuck)

snob, snobbery, snobbish, snobbishness

snow, snowfall, snowflake, snowflurries
snowstorm

Snowbirds (Canadian Forces flying team)

snowbirds (Canadians who winter in the South)

snowmobile (*one word*)

snowshoe, snowshoer

s.o.b. (Editors' Note required when spelled out:
son of a bitch)

sober

Sobeys Inc.

Social Credit party

Social Crediter (*not* -or)

socialism, socialist (philosophical attitude)

Socialist (party or member)

Société franco-manitobaine, la

society, Audubon Society

Socred (*n.* and *adj.*)

softpedal (*not* -peddle)

soft-spoken (*hyphen*)

software

softy, softies

Solberg, Monte (politician)

Soleil, Le (Quebec)

solicitor general, solicitors general

solo, solos

soluble

Solzhenitsyn, Alexander

Somali (*n.*), Somalian (*adj.*)

sombre (*not* -er)

some, someday, someplace, somebody,
somebodies, somehow, someone,
something, at some time (*two words*),
sometime (*adv.*; also *adj.*, former — *one
word*), somewhat, somewhere

Somers, Harry (composer, 1925-99)

somersault

S

soprano, sopranos
SOS (*no periods*)
Sotheby's Canada Inc.
    –Sotheby's for short
South–Capitalize regions *but not* their
    derivatives. Lowercase mere direction or
    position.
    –the South (region of Canada, United States, etc.)
    –a southerner
    –Southern California
    –Southern Canada
    –southern Canadian markets
    –southern prices
    –south of the border
    –to go south
    –the Deep South (U.S.)
    –a southern accent
    –southern states (U.S.)
    –The South lost to the North.
    –the southern army
    –the South Pacific
    –southern Ireland
Southam Fellowships
    –a Southam Fellow
Southam Inc.
Southam News
South Asian (*not* East Indian)
South Carolina (S.C.)
South Dakota (S.D.)
southeast (*one word*)
    –Southeast Asia Treaty Organization (SEATO)
Southern Canada, southern Canadian weather
southern France
Southern Hemisphere
southern Ontario
southern states (U.S.)
South Pole, the Pole
sou'wester (waterproof hat)
sovereigntist (*not* sovereignist)

S

sovereignty-association

Soviet Union, former (Union of Soviet
   Socialist Republics, U.S.S.R.)

soybean, soy sauce

Space–Use arabic numerals for spacecraft and
   launch vehicles: Sputnik 1, Apollo 11,
   Gemini 5, Alouette 2. *But* Anik A, Anik B.

Spanish Civil War

Spartan

Speaker —Capitalize in all references to avoid
   ambiguity.
      –Speaker Martha Lim, the Speaker
      –deputy Speaker Glenn Eckert, the
      deputy Speaker, former Speaker

spectre (*not* -er)

speech from the throne

speed skater, speed skating

spellbinder (*no hyphen*)

sphinx (winged monster)

Sphinx (representation near pyramids)

Spielberg, Steven

spina bifida

spin off (*v.*), spinoff (*n. and adj.*)

splendour

spoonful, spoonfuls

sport utility vehicle (*not* sports; SUV *but avoid*)

spring (season)

squadron leader (*no abbvn.*)

Squid-Jiggin' Ground, the (Newfoundland ballad)

Srebrenica (Bosnia)

Sri Lanka, Sri Lankan
      –Sri Lanka Freedom party

SS (steamship)

SS (Schutzstaffel, Nazi elite guard)

stadium, stadiums

staff, staffs (poles), staves (music)

staff inspector, Staff Insp. Albert Dupont

staff sergeant (Staff Sgt.)

Stalin, Josef (1879-1953)

S

stampede, Calgary Stampede, the Stampede
Standard and Poor's Corp.
standardbred, thoroughbred
standard time
—eastern, central, mountain standard time
—Atlantic, Pacific daylight time
—MST, EDT (*not* EDST)
stand by (*v.*), standby (*n.*), standbys
stand in (*v.*), stand-in (*n.*)
stand off (*v.*), standoff (*n.*)
Stand Off, Alta.
stand out (*v.*), standout (*n.*)
Stanley Cup
Star (*not* Star!) specialty channel
Stars and Stripes
startup (*n* and *adj.*)
state, New York state (geog.)
—State of New York (corp.)
—*but* in the state of New York
—state of the union message
Station—Capitalize as important building *but*
not when known by name of railway or
town.
—Union Station
—the Via Rail station
—Leaside station
stationary (not moving)
stationery (writing materials)
Statistics Canada (*no abbvn.*)
STD (sexually transmitted disease)
steelworker
Stefansson, Vilhjalmur (explorer, 1879-1962)
Steinem, Gloria (feminist)
Stelco Inc. (Steel Co. of Canada Ltd.)
Stephenson, Sir William (1896-1989)
stepdaughter, stepson, stepmother, stepfather
but step-parent
stepping-stone (*hyphen*)
Stetson (trademark)

still life, still lifes
stimulus, stimuli
stock exchange, Toronto Stock Exchange
stock market
stockpile (*one word*)
STOL (short takeoff and landing)
Stone Age
Stoney band (Alberta Indians), Stoneys
Stoney Creek, Ont. and N.B.
stony (*not* stoney)
Stony Lake (near Peterborough, Ont.)
Stony Mountain, Man.
Stony Plain, Alta.
storey (building), storeys
storm, hailstorm, rainstorm, snowstorm
strafe, strafing
Strahl, Chuck (politician)
straightforward (*no hyphen*)
Strait–Capitalize when used with names.
     –Strait of Juan de Fuca
     –Georgia Strait
straitjacket
straitlaced
stratagem, stratagems
Stratas, Teresa (soprano)
strategic arms limitation talks (SALT)
     –SALT I, SALT II
Stratford Beacon Herald
Stratford Festival (*not* Stratford Shakespearean Festival)
     –*but* Stratford Shakespearean Festival
     Foundation of Canada
     –American Shakespeare Theatre (in Connecticut)
Stratford upon Avon
     –STRATFORD UPON AVON
     (in placelines)
stratum, strata
streamline (*one word*)

Street–Capitalize when used with names;
abbreviate in numbered street addresses.
- –Bay Street, Wall Street
- –along Queen Street East
- –10 Queen St. E.
- –*but* 10 Downing Street
(official residence)

streetcar (*one word*)

Streisand, Barbra

streptococcus, streptococci
- –*but* strep throat

strikebound (*no hyphen*)

strikebreaker (generally editorial; *use advisedly*)

striptease

strongman

strontium-90

Styrofoam (trademark for a plastic foam)

suave, suavely, suaveness, suavity, suavities

subcommittee (*no hyphen*)

subcompact

sub judice (*two words, but avoid*)

sub-lieutenant (Sub-Lieut.)

submachine-gun

subpoena (*n.* and *v.*), subpoenas,
subpoenaed, subpoenaing

subtle
subtlety, subtleties

succinct, succinctly

suffered (*not* sustained) injury

suffragan (bishop)

Sukkot (Jewish festival)

sulfa drugs

sulphide, sulphite, sulphur

summer (season)

summerfallow

Summerside Journal-Pioneer

summit, summit conference (heads of government)

summons, summonses
summonsed (to appear in court)
sun
Suncor Energy Inc .
Super Bowl
supercilious (*not* -silious)
superintendent, Supt. Herman Frank
supermarket (*one word*)
supersede
suppress, suppression, suppressor
supremacist (*not* supremist)
Supreme Court (federal, provincial, state)
Sûreté du Québec
      (*prefer* Quebec provincial police)
Suriname
Suzuki, David (geneticist)
SUV (sport utility vehicle, *but avoid*)
swap (*not* swop)
SWAT (special weapons and tactics) team
sweatshirt
sweepstake
      –Irish hospitals sweepstakes
      –the sweep
sweeten, sweetener, sweetening
Sydney, N.S., and Australia, *but* Sidney, B.C.
Sydney Cape Breton Post
Sydney Steel Corp. (Sysco)
syllabus, syllabuses
symbol, symbolize
symmetrical, symmetry
symphony, Tchaikovsky's Fourth Symphony
symposium, symposiums
synagogue, Holy Blossom Synagogue
syndrome, Reye's, Down
synod, Anglican synod
      –Lutheran Church – Missouri Synod
      (denom.)
      –Orthodox Holy synod (Istanbul)
syphilis

Syrah (grape)
syrup (*not* sirup)
Sysco (Sydney Steel Corp.)

T

T, *as in* to a T
Tabasco (trademark for a hot sauce)
tableau, tableaus
taekwondo (*one word*)
Tai Chi (*two words*)
Taipei
Tajikistan, Tajik
take off (*v.*), takeoff. (*n.*)
take out (*v.*), takeout (*n.*)
take over (*v.*), takeover (*n.*)
taken (*not* rushed) to hospital
tangelo, tangelos
tank, M-60, PT-76, Leopard 1
targeted
tariff, Tariff Act
        –General Agreement on Tariffs and Trade (GATT)
Taser (weapon)
task force (military term; *avoid overuse*)
Tass (See Itar-Tass)
tassel, tasselled
T-ball
tattoo, tattooed
Tchaikovsky, Peter (1840-1893)
teammate (*no hyphen*)
Teamsters union (acceptable in all references to the
        International Brotherhood of Teamsters, Chauffeurs,
        Warehousemen and Helpers of America), a teamster
        (member of the union)
tear gas (*two words*)
technical sergeant (Tech. Sgt.)
Technicolor (trademark for a process of
        making colour movies)
teenage (*adj.*), teenager, teens
teeny-bopper
teepee
teetotal, teetotaller, teetotalism
Teflon (trademark for a non-stick coating)
Tehran
telecommunication

Telephone numbers–Use hyphen, not brackets
   or spaces to break up:
   1-519-228-6262,
   1-800-268-9237.
TelePrompTer (trademark)
Telesat Canada
Teletype (trademark for teleprinter)
Telex (trade name)
telltale (*no hyphen*)
Telstar (satellite)
Temagami, Ont. (*not* Tim-)
Témiscaming, Que. (town)
Témiscamingue (Que. county, electoral district)
Ten Commandments
   –Second Commandment
tendency (*not* -ancy), tendencies
tendon, Achilles tendon, *but* tendinitis
ten-gallon hat
Tennant, Veronica (ballet)
Tennessee (Tenn.)
tenpins (bowling)
tenterhooks (*not* tender-)
Teresa, Mother (1910-1997)
terminus, terminuses
testament, Old Testament
Test match (cricket, rugby)
   –England-Australia Test match
   –the Test
Texas (Tex.)
textbook
thalidomide
Thanksgiving Day (Canada, second Monday
   in October; U.S., last Thursday in November)
The Associated Press (AP)
   –The Associated Press says ...
   –*but* the Associated Press reporter
Theatre–Capitalize as important buildings.
   –National Arts Centre
   –Princess of Wales Theatre

The Canadian Press (CP)
>   –The Canadian Press says ...
>   –*but* the Canadian Press reporter

The Hague

the (*lowercase*) Netherlands
>   –UTRECHT, Netherlands (placeline)

The Pas, Man.

therapeutic

thesis, theses

the West Indies

think-tank

Third World

Thompson, Greg (politician)

Thompson, Myron (politician)

Thomson Corp. (international parent company)
>   –Thomson Newspapers Co. Ltd.
>   –the Thomson group of newspapers

Thomson, Ken (*but* Lord Thomson of Fleet
>   in the United Kingdom)
>   –Roy Thomson Hall (Toronto)

Thomson, R.H. (actor)

Thomson, Tom (painter, 1877-1917)

thoroughbred, standardbred

Thousand Islands (Ontario)

3-D

Three Wise Men

threshold

throne speech, speech from the throne

Thunder Bay Chronicle-Journal

Tiananmen Square

tick-tack-toe (game)

tidbit

tie, tying

tiebreaker (game)

tie up (*v.*), tie-up (*n.*)

till, until, *not* 'til

time, daylight, standard
>   –eastern daylight time (EDT)
>   –Pacific standard time (PST)

–7 a.m., 6 p.m., 12:30 p.m.

Time magazine

Times (of London), the

time-slot

Tim Hortons (*no apostrophe*)
>–a Tim Hortons shop

Timiskaming (Ontario lake and district)

Timiskaming-Cochrane (federal riding in Ontario)

Timiskaming Indian reserve (Quebec)

Timorese (*n.* and *adj.*)

Titles–Capitalize formal titles when preceding names, not when following or when set off by commas: Judge John Jones; a judge, John Jones, spoke. But lowercase titles used with former, onetime, -elect, designate and similar adjectives, as former president Hoover, former prime minister Brian Mulroney, prime minister-designate John Smith. Lowercase mere occupation (GM president John Smith, bus driver Mary Brown) and in sport stories (captain John Brown).

Tkachuk, David (senator)

TNT (trinitrotoluene)

to a T

T.O. (nickname for Toronto)

toboggan

tomato, tomatoes

ton (2,000 pounds), long ton (2,240 pounds), tonne (1,000 kilograms or 2,204.62 pounds)
>–Use ton, not tonne, in colloquial references (he weighed a ton; fell like a ton of bricks).

toonie, toonies ($2 coin)

top-notch (*adj.*)

toque — *Use* tuque

tornado, tornadoes

Toronto Dominion Bank, TD Bank

Toronto St. Michael's Majors (hockey team)

Torstar Corp.

total, totalled

Touch-Tone (trademark for push-button dialling)

T

tourniquet
tower, CN Tower, Eiffel Tower
town, Town of Elmira (corp.)
    –but in the town of Elmira
township, Wilmot Township
    –but in the township of Wilmot
Toys "R" Us
trademark, trade name
traffic, trafficker, trafficking
traitor, traitorous
tranquillity
tranquillizer
Transalta Corp.
transatlantic, transpacific
Trans-Canada Highway
TransCanada PipeLines Ltd.
transcontinental (*no hyphen*)
transfer, transferred
Transkei (former homeland state in South Africa)
translator (*not* -er)
transpacific
Trans World Airlines Inc. (TWA)
trauma, traumas, traumatic
travel, traveller, traveller's cheques
Treasury Board
treaty, Columbia River Treaty
    –Treaty 6 (*not* Six)
Tremblay, Stephan (politician)
tremor
Tribune, La (newspaper in Sherbrooke, Que.)
Trilon Financial Corp.
Trimark Financial Corp.
triple-A rating (bonds, baseball)
Triple Crown (horse racing)
triple-decker
Triple-E Senate
TriStar (Lockheed aircraft)
Trivial Pursuit (trademark board game)
Trizec Hahn Corp.

T

Trois-Rivières, Que.
trooper (military, *no abbvn.*), trouper
    (a staunch colleague – a "real trouper")
Trophy–Capitalize specific names.
    –Vézina Trophy
    –a championship trophy
Trudeau, Pierre Elliott (1919-2000)
Truman, Harry S. (1884-1972)
trustee, trustee Joanne Rocci
Tsawwassen, B.C.
T-shirt
tsunami (wave)
Tsuu T'ina Nation (aboriginal band)
tug of war (*no hyphens*)
Tuktoyaktuk, N.W.T.
tumour *but* tumorous
tupek (Inuit equivalent of teepee, wigwam)
tuque (knitted cap)
turkey, turkeys
Turkmenistan
Turp, Daniel (politician)
turtleneck sweater (*no hyphen*)
Tussaud's, Madame (waxworks in London)
    –*but* Louis Tussaud's (waxworks at
    Niagara Falls, Ont.)
Tutankhamen
Tutor (training jet)
TVA Group Inc.
TV Dinner (trademark for frozen dinner)
TVOntario
tweezer, pair of tweezers
Twelfth Night
Twelve Apostles, the
20th Century-Fox
twentysomething (*one word*)
two, twos
tying (*not* tieing)
typeface
typhoon Alice

U-boat
UFO(s) for unidentified flying object(s)
Ukraine (*not* the Ukraine)
Ukrainian
ultimatum, ultimatums
ultrasound
Ultrasuede (trademark for a mock suede)
ultra vires (beyond the powers, *but avoid*)
umiak (Inuit open boat)
Umlaut–Indicate in German names by placing
     letter "e" after vowel affected.
     –Goebbels for Göbbels
     –Duesseldorf for Düsseldorf
unabomber (Theodore Kaczynski)
unchristian, *but* non-Christian
unco-operative
unco-ordinated
underprivileged
undersecretary (*one word*)
underway
unforeseen
unforgivable (*not* -eable)
uninterested (not interested), disinterested (impartial)
UNICEF (OK in first reference)
union, state of the union message
Union Jack
Union Nationale
Union of Soviet Socialist Republics, former
     (U.S.S.R., Soviet Union)
United Appeal campaign
United Church of Canada
United Kingdom–England, Scotland, Wales
     and Northern Ireland. But use "British
     government" and such in preference to
     "United Kingdom government."
United Nations (UN)
     –Food and Agriculture Organization of
     the United Nations (FAO, *but avoid*)
     –General Assembly

U

–International Bank for Reconstruction
and Development (World Bank)
–International Civil Aviation
Organization (ICAO)
–International Court of Justice (*no abbvn.*)
–International Labour Organization (ILO)
–International Monetary Fund (IMF)
–Security Council
–United Nations Children's Fund,
formerly UN International Children's
Emergency Fund (UNICEF)
–United Nations Disaster Relief
Organization (UNDRO, *but avoid*)
–United Nations Educational, Scientific
and Cultural Organization (UNESCO)
–World Health Organization (WHO)

Unitel Communications Inc.
(formerly CNCP Telecommunications)

University–Capitalize the names of universities
and colleges.
–Memorial University
–Simon Fraser University
–Cariboo College
–Regis College
Lowercase departments, programs and courses.
–political science department
–natives studies course
–faculty of education

University Degrees–Lowercase except when
abbreviated.
–bachelor of arts (BA), a bachelor's
degree
–master of arts (MA)
–master of science (M.Sc.)
–doctor of philosophy (PhD)
Avoid using unfamiliar abbreviations for degrees.

Unknown Soldier
unmistakable (*not* -eable)
unshakable (*not* -eable)

unwieldy
Upper Canada (region; name for Ontario 1791-1841)
upper house, chamber
Upstate New York
URL (uniform or universal resource locator)
US (use only with dollar figures: $550 US)
usable (*not* useable)
usage (*not* useage)
USAir Inc.
USA Today
usurer, usurious, usury
Utah (no abbvn.)
Utopia
  —but a utopia
U-turn
Uzbekistan

V

vacillate

vacuum

Val-d'Isère

valentine (card)
> –*but* Valentine's Day

Valhalla

Valium (trademark for a tranquillizer)

Valkyrie

valley, Fraser Valley

valour *but* valorous

Van, Von–When lowercase in names,
> capitalize only at start of sentences. Van
> in Vietnamese names is uppercase.

Vanclief, Lyle (politician)

Vancouver Grizzlies (basketball)

Van Doo (nickname of Quebec's Royal 22nd
Regiment)
> –Van Doos (personnel of the regiment)
> –Van Doo (one member)

van Gogh, Vincent (1853-1890)

Vanier, Georges (1888-1967)

vapour, vapourish *but* vaporous

Vaseline (trademark for a petroleum jelly)

Vatican II, Second Vatican Council

vaudeville

V-chip (television)

VCR (OK in first reference for video cassette recorder)

Veda (scripture of Hinduism)

VE-Day, VJ-Day

Velcro (trademark)

Venne, Pierrette (politician)

venetian blind

ventilator (*not* respirator)

veranda (*not* -ah)

verbatim (*not* -um)

Vermilion, Alta.

Vermont (Vt.)

Versus–Use the abbreviation vs. only in
> sports schedules, agate and the names of court cases.

V

vertebra, vertebrae
veterinarian
Vézina Trophy
Viagra (impotence drug)
Via Rail (*not* VIA)
vice (bad habit), vise (clamp)
vice-admiral (*no abbvn.*)
vice-president
      –U.S. Vice-President James Smith
      –former U.S. vice-president Walter
      Mondale
      –GM vice-president Joan Arthur
vice versa (*two words*)
vichyssoise
vicious
Vickers, Jon (tenor)
Victoria Cross (VC)
Victoria Times Colonist
video, video cassette, video cassette recorder (VCR
      acceptable in first reference), videotape (*no abbvn.*)
Videotron Groupe Ltd.
vie, *but* vying
Vietnam, Vietnamese
vigour, vigorous
vilify
village, Village of Bridgeport (corp.)
      –*but* in the village of Bridgeport
VIP (for Very Important Person), VIPs
Virgin (Christ's mother)
Virginia (Va.)
Virgin Islands (*no abbvn.*)
virtuoso, virtuosos
Visa (credit card)
vis-a-vis
viscount, Viscount Montgomery
viscous (sticky)
vise (clamp), vice (bad habit)
Vishnu
vitamin B

V

Vizinczey, Stephen (novelist)
V-neck
vociferous
Voice of Women (VoW)
Voisey's Bay (Labrador)
Voix de l'Est, La (newspaper in Granby, Que.)
volatile
volcano, volcanoes
Volkswagen
vomit, vomited, vomiting
Von, Van–When lowercase in names,
        capitalize only at start of sentence. Van
        in Vietnamese names is uppercase.
        –von Hassel, Kai-Uwe (Germany)
        –von Thadden, Adolf (Germany)
vow (solemn oath; often misused)
vs. (abbreviation for versus, used only in
        sports schedules, agate and the names of
        court cases)

W

wacky (*not* whacky)
wagon, bandwagon, chuckwagon, station wagon
Walesa, Lech
walkie-talkie
Walkman (trademark for headset stereo)
walk out (*v.*), walkout (*n.*)
Walkuere, Die (Wagner opera)
wall, Berlin Wall, Great Wall of China,
        Wailing Wall (in Jerusalem; prefer
        Western Wall), Wall Street
Wal-Mart
War–Capitalize major armed conflicts.
        –Civil War (U.S.)
        –First World War (*not* World War I)
        –Persian Gulf War
        –Second World War (*not* World War II)
        –*but* a third world war
        –Six-Day War
        –Korean War
        –Vietnam War
        –Wars of the Roses
        –cod war
        –tariff war
        –Cold War (fanciful term)
Ward 2
warhorse, warlord, warmonger
Warner Bros.
warrant officer (*no abbvn.*)
        –chief warrant officer
        –master warrant officer
Warsaw Pact, former
wartime
Washington, D.C.
Washington (Wash.)
WASP (white Anglo-Saxon Protestant)
Wassermann test
wastebasket
Wasylycia-Leis, Judy (politician)
watchdog

waterfowl

Waterloo, University of (*not* Waterloo University)

water-ski, water-skiing

wavelength

Web site, master, page

Week–Capitalize special events, as Apple Week.

weekday, weekend (*one word*)

weird, weirdo

Welch (regiment names)

    –but Welsh Guards

Welland Canal

well-being (*hyphen*)

Welsh (folk, tongue)

welsh (on a bet; *avoid*)

Welshpool, N.B. (*not* Welch-)

West–Capitalize regions but not their

    derivatives. Lowercase mere direction or

    position.

    –the West (region)

    –The West won the Grey Cup.

    –a westerner

    –one western MP

    –Western Canada

    –a western Canadian

    –the western Canadian provinces

    –the western provinces

    –western premiers

    –in western Manitoba

    –The snow moves west across Western

    Canada.

    –West Coast (region)

    –west coast (shoreline)

    –the East-West talks

    –western Europe

    –western leaders

    –western France

    –Western Hemisphere

    –the richest countries in the West

    –the richest western countries

West Bank (of the River Jordan)
West End (London theatre district)
western (movie)
Westjet Airlines Ltd.
Westminster (London), New Westminster, B.C.
Westmorland County (N.B. and England)
West Virginia (W.Va.)
West, Wild
Weston, Hilary
Weyerhaeuser Co. Ltd.
W-Five
wharf, wharfs
Wheat–Capitalize varieties generally except where
    usage has established the lowercase;
    Selkirk, *but* durum.
wheelchair
whereabouts (usually takes a singular verb)
whip, party whip John O'Neill
whisky, whiskies (*never* whiskey)
Whitehorse, Yukon
White House
white paper (a report issued by government
    to provide information)
whiz, whiz-kid
whodunit (*not* -nn-)
Whycocomagh (First Nations band on Cape Breton)
-wide, worldwide, provincewide, countrywide
    (*avoid* nationwide when countrywide is meant)
wield
wiener, wiener schnitzel
wigwag (*no hyphen*)
Wild West
Wilfrid Laurier University
wilful (*not* willful)
Wimbledon tennis championships
wing commander (Wing Cmdr.)
winter (season)
Winter Olympic Games, the Winter Games, the Games
Wisconsin (Wis.)

wit, halfwit, halfwitted
   –at his wit's end
withdraw, withdrawal
withhold
woman–Don't use as an adjective unless man would
   be used in similar fashion (womenswear,
   menswear). *Prefer* female if it is necessary
   to specify sex.
   –female lawyer, *not* woman lawyer
Woman's Christian Temperance Union (*not* Women's)
womenswear, menswear
woollen, woolly
word processor, word processing
Workers Compensation Board (*no apostrophe* in
   Prince Edward Island, Manitoba)
Workers' Compensation Board (*with
   apostrophe* in British Columbia, Alberta,
   Nova Scotia, Newfoundland and Saskatchewan)
Workers' Compensation, Health and Safety
   Board (Yukon)
Workplace Health, Safety and Compensation
   Commission (New Brunswick)
Workplace Safety and Insurance Board (Ontario)
workforce
workload
workplace
world
   –Old World, New World
   –free world (*but avoid*)
   –Third World
World Bank
World Cup (soccer)
World Health Organization (WHO)
World Series (baseball), the Series
world's fair, Montreal, New York
   –Canadian World Exhibition
   (official name)
   –Expo 67, Expo 86 (*no apostrophe*)
worldwide (*one word*)

World Wide Web, the Web, Web site
worshippers
worthwhile
write off (*v.*), writeoff (*n.*)
wrongdoer, wrongdoing, wrongful
Wyoming (Wyo.)

Xerox (trademark for a photocopier, etc.)
Xinhua (New China news agency)
X chromosome, Y chromosome
X-Files, The
X-rated (movie)
X-ray (*n.* and *v.*)
yahoo
Yahoo Inc. (*not* Yahoo! Inc.)
Yahweh
Yamani, Sheik Ahmed Zaki
Yangon (formerly Rangoon)
Yankee
yarmulke (skullcap)
Year, Man of the, Newsmaker of the
Yellowhead Pass
yenta
Y-Flyer (sailboat)
YMCA (Young Men's Christian Association)
yogurt
Yom Kippur
Young Women's Christian Association (YWCA)
Yugoslavia, Yugoslav
Yukon, the
         –but Yukon in placelines: FARO, Yukon
yule, yuletide
yuppie
(young urban professional)
Zaire (now Congo)
Zamboni
(trademark for ice-surfacing machine)
Zellers (*no apostrophe*)
Zen-Buddhism
zero, zeros
zigzag (*no hyphen*)
Zimbabwe
Zinfandel
Zion, Zionism, Zionist
zip code (U.S.)
Znaimer, Moses (television)

X-Y-Z

zodiac
zoologist, zoology
zucchini

Act 1, the first act
Article 8, Art. 8
behind the 8-ball
Big Five banks
Big Three automakers
Category 3
CBC Radio One, Radio Two
Cdn (used only with dollar figures:
    $1,386 Cdn)
Cell Block 5
cents, nine cents, 43 cents
Channel 2 (television)
Chapter 2
Cloud 9
Day 1
VIII (*no period*)
55 BC; AD 1978
four-by-four (four-wheel-drive vehicle)
4-for-5 (four hits in five at-bats)
4-H
Fractions–Use figures for all numbers with
    fractions (9 3/4). Spell out and hyphenate
    common fractions used alone (three-quarters).
Grade 7
Latitude, longitude – 44 degrees north, 49
    degrees 30 minutes west, etc.
Leopard 1 (tank)
line 46
1984 (movie version of Orwell novel Nineteen Eighty-Four)
1930s, '30s
    –but Expo 67, Expo 86 (*no apostrophe*)
No. 1, number 1 (*not* number one)
page 23, p. 23
paragraph 3
Phase 2
Room 14
Round 3
Scene 3, the third scene
Section 8, Sec. 8

Numbers

7Up (soft drink)
Square 1, back to
Telephone numbers–Use hyphens,
      not spaces or brackets to break up:
     416-228-6262, 1-888-268-9237
360networks Inc.
10 Downing Street (*exception*)
24 Sussex Drive (*exception*)
10th (*no period*)
Treaty 6
20th century
20th Century-Fox
two-by-four
49th parallel
2,4-D (weed killer)
US (used only with dollar figures: $295 US)
V-6, V-8 (engine)
verse 3
Y2K (for the year 2000)

Plain Words

When there is a choice of words, prefer the short to the long, the familiar to the unfamiliar. This chapter lists some long or formal words along with some shorter or more familiar alternatives that may do the job better.

abandon	leave, quit, give up
abbreviate	shorten, cut
abduct	kidnap, seize
abolish	end, do away with, scrap
abrasion	scrape, scratch
accelerate	hurry, speed up
accessible	easily reached, ready, at hand
accommodate	house, shelter, put up
accordingly	so, therefore
according to	under; say
accumulate	pile up, collect
acknowledge	admit, concede
acquire	buy, gain, get
acquit	free, clear, release
additional	added, more, extra
in addition to	besides
adhere	stick, cling
adjacent	beside, next to, touching
administer	manage, direct, control
adverse	harmful, damaging
advise	tell, write, inform
advocate	support, call for
affluent	rich, well-to-do
aggravate	annoy, provoke, worsen
aggressive	pushing, pushy
alienate	put off, turn against
allegiance	loyalty
alleviate	ease, soften
alteration	change, revision
alternate	take turns
alternative	choice, other
amalgamate	unite, combine
amendment	change, revision
amicable	friendly, pleasant

Plain Words

anonymous	nameless, unknown
antagonize	offend, anger
apparent	clear, plain, obvious
appreciative	grateful, thankful
appropriate	fit, proper
approximately	about
aptitude	gift, knack, talent
arguably	perhaps, maybe
as far as...	
is concerned	as to
asphyxiate	choke, suffocate
assist	help, aid
astute	shrewd, clever
attempt	try
attired	dressed, wearing
authentic	genuine, real, true
authorize	approve, allow, give power
autonomous	free, independent, self-governing
available	ready, on hand
bargain	deal
beneficial	good for, helpful, useful
bereavement	death, loss
beverage	drink
biannual	twice a year, every two years
bigotry	bias, narrow-mindedness, racism
bilateral	two-sided
bona fide	real, in good faith
capacity	ability, position, space, size
catastrophe	disaster
cease	stop, end
censure	blame, scold
characteristic	trait, mark, feature
circumstance	event, condition, fact
clad	dressed, wearing
coagulate	clot, congeal
coerce	force, press
collaborate	work together, team up

comatose	unconscious
commence	begin, start
commitment	promise, pledge
communicable	catching, infectious
communicate	tell, inform, write, telephone
comparable	like, similar
compensate	pay, make up
competent	able, trained
complete	fill out, finish
complimentary	free
comply	follow, obey, give in
compulsion	urge
conceive	think up, imagine, dream up
concerning	about, for, on
conclude	end
concur	agree, match
conduct	carry on, do, run
confederation	alliance, league, union
congenital	inborn, inbred
conscientious	careful, painstaking
consequently	so
considerable	much, ample
consolation	comfort, relief, help
conspicuous	plain, obvious
constitute	are, make up, form
construct	build, make
consult	ask, talk over
consume	eat, use up
contaminate	taint, pollute, dirty, poison
contemplate	consider, study, weigh
contribute	give, share, help
controversy	debate, issue
contusion	bruise
convenient	useful, handy
convulsion	seizure, spasm
corroborate	confirm, verify
counterfeit	false, phoney, fake
courteous	polite

Plain Words

criterion	test, rule, model, yardstick
currently	now
deactivate	shut off, close
dearth	lack, shortage, scarcity
deceased	dead
decompose	rot, decay
decontaminate	purify, disinfect, sterilize
decrease	cut, drop, fall
decry	blame, condemn
de-emphasize	play down, softpedal
de facto	actual, real
defective	faulty, broken
deficient	lacking, poor
defraud	cheat, swindle, fleece
demonstrate	show, prove
depart	go, leave, check out
deplete	empty, sap, reduce
depreciate	lessen, cheapen, scorn
depressed	backward, diminished; sad
designate	name, call, label
destitute	poor, needy, bare
determine	fix, test, find out, decide, settle
development	growth, change
deviate	swerve, stray, turn aside, vary
dimension	size
diminutive	tiny
disallow	turn down, reject
discontinue	end, give up, stop
disembark	get off, leave, land
disguise	hide, mask
disintegrate	fall apart, crumble, break up
dispatch	send, issue
display	show, bare
distinguish	tell apart, make out
distribute	hand out, spread

divulge	tell, give, reveal
don	put on, get into
donation	gift, present
draconian	harsh
dubious	unsure, doubtful
duplicate	copy, repeat
dwell	live, occupy
eccentric	odd, strange
economical	thrifty, cheap
edifice	building
elevate	lift, raise
eliminate	get rid of, throw out, drop
emaciated	gaunt, bony, thin, wasted
eminent	famous, high, noted
emphasize	stress, underline
empirical	practical
employ	use, hire, apply
encounter	meet, come upon
endorsement	support, backing
enhance	add to, improve
ensue	follow, develop
enumerate	count, add up, cite
envisage	see, foresee, imagine
escalate	step up, intensify
eschew	avoid
in the event of	if
evident	plain, obvious
excessive	too much, undue
in excess of	over
exhibit	show, reveal, display
exonerate	free, clear, acquit
exorbitant	excessive, too high, overpriced
expedite	speed up, push
expenditure	spending, expense, cost
experience	feel, live through, undergo
expertise	skill, knowledge, know-how

Plain Words

explicit	clear, precise, exact
extended	long, drawn out
extensive	large, wide, broad, roomy
exterminate	wipe out, destroy
extinguish	put out, douse, smother
fabricate	make, build; lie, trump up
facilitate	ease, make easy, help, lighten
failed to	did not
fallacy	error, fault, pitfall
feasible	possible, can be done, workable
finalize	finish, complete, end
fluctuate	rise and fall, swing, waver
fortunate	lucky, happy
fracture	break
frequently	often
frustration	defeat, dismay
fundamental	basic, real
generate	produce, cause
gratuity	gift, tip
on the grounds that	because
hazardous	unsafe, risky, dangerous
ideology	beliefs
illumination	light, insight
illustration	example, picture, drawing
immediately	at once, now
immense	huge, vast
immovable	set, firm, fixed
impartial	neutral, fair, just
impeccable	flawless, perfect
impede	slow, hamper, stall, hinder
imperative	urgent, vital, pressing
imperceptible	slight, subtle, hidden
impersonate	copy, mimic
impetus	spur, push, urge

Plain Words

implement	do, set up, begin, carry out
impolite	rude
impostor	cheat, fraud, ringer
impotent	weak, helpless, powerless
inaccuracy	mistake, error
inadvertent	accidental, careless
inadvisable	unwise, risky
inaugurate	begin, launch
in camera	private
incapacitate	disable, damage, lay up
incarcerate	jail, intern, imprison
incision	cut, slit
incite	rouse, prod, goad
inclement	stormy, harsh, nasty
incompetent	unfit, inept
incomprehensible	baffling
inconceivable	incredible, beyond belief
incorrect	wrong
increase	rise, go up, gain, grow
incredulous	dubious, skeptical
indefinite	vague, uncertain, dim
independent	free; well-off
indicate	show, suggest, hint, imply
indigenous	native
indignant	angry, upset
indispensable	vital, crucial, essential
individual	person, man, woman
ineligible	unfit, unsuitable
inevitable	sure, destined
inexpensive	cheap, low-priced, modest
inflexible	rigid, firm, stiff
inform	tell
ingenious	clever, deft, masterly
inherent	inborn, inbred, essential
inhibit	check, hinder, curb
initial	first
initiate	begin, open
injunction	ban, order

Plain Words

in lieu of	instead of
innate	inborn, natural
innovation	change, novelty
input	say, opinion, suggestion
inquire	ask
insecure	unsafe, unsure
institute	set up, begin, found
instrument	tool, agent, means
insufficient	not enough, short
insurrection	revolt, riot, mutiny
integrate	absorb, combine, mix
intention	aim, plan, goal, purpose
interface	work together, connect
intermission	pause, break
interrogate	question, pump, quiz
interrupt	break in, butt in, hinder, stop
intersection	corner
inundate	flood, deluge, overflow, engulf
irrelevant	beside the point, off-base
irresponsible	careless, rash, reckless
jurisdiction	control, power, domain
laceration	cut, tear, gash
latitude	scope, range
laud	praise
lenient	mild, gentle, sparing
liberate	free, rescue
locality	place, spot, site
locate	find, pinpoint
lubricate	oil, grease
magnitude	size, extent
majority	most, bulk, mass
manufacture	make, produce, build
maximum	most, biggest, longest
meaningful	big, important, significant
medication	medicine, remedy, pill, drug
mediocre	ordinary, run-of-the-mill
mentality	mind, frame of mind, outlook

methodology	method
milieu	setting, scene; culture
minimal	small, token
minimize	lessen, play down, belittle, diminish
minuscule	tiny
mitigate	ease, soften, make mild, temper
modification	change
momentous	important
motivate	inspire, drive, cause
narrate	tell, recount, relate
nauseous	sickening, repulsive
necessitate	need, compel, call for
negligent	careless
negotiate	bargain, talk business
neo-natal	newborn
neophyte	novice, beginner, learner, apprentice
neutralize	offset, cancel
nominal	small, token
notification	notice, warning
numerous	many
nurture	feed, train
nutritious	nourishing, wholesome
objective	end, aim, goal, mission
obligation	duty, debt
oblige	compel, force
obscure	dim, hidden
observation	remark, comment
obsolescent	dying out, disappearing
obsolete	worn-out, disused, out-of-date
obstruction	barrier, block, hurdle
obtain	get, come by, gain
occasion	event, cause, chance
occupation	job, trade, profession
occurrence	event, incident
ongoing	continuing, active, permanent

Plain Words

operate	work, run; cut out, remove
opportunity	chance
optimal	best
option	choice
originate	invent, create
outrageous	shocking, disgusting
overabundance	abundance, excess, glut
overview	view, survey
palatable	tasty, pleasing, sweet
panache	dash, pizzazz, zip
parameter	limit, boundary
paraphrase	reword, restate
parochial	narrow
participate	take part, share in, join in
pending	until, in the air
perceive	see, view, regard
periphery	edge, outskirts
permanent	lasting, endless
permission	consent, go-ahead
perquisite	perk, fringe benefit, right
persevere	persist, hold on, endure, stand
perspiration	sweat
persuade	win over, sway, coax
pertinent	fit, right, apt
philosophy	idea, view, system
physician	doctor
place	put
pollute	dirty, poison, taint
portion	part, piece, share
position	job
possess	own, have
postpone	put off, shelve, delay
practicable	workable, can be done
pragmatic	practical
preclude	prevent, shut out, avert
predicament	difficulty
prejudicial	harmful
preliminary to	before

Plain Words

preparedness	readiness
prerogative	privilege, right
presently	soon
prestigious	honoured, famous
principal	main, chief
prior to	before
probability	likelihood, chance
procedure	way, course, method
proceed	go
proficient	skilled, deft, masterly
prohibit	ban, prevent, forbid
project	plan
proliferation	spread
prophesy	foretell, predict
proponent	advocate, supporter
proposal	plan, offer
prosthesis	artificial limb
protocol	etiquette, usage
provide	give, offer, have, say
proviso	condition
provoke	stir up, annoy, tease
prowess	skill, talent
purchase	buy
for the purpose of	to
qualification	ability, skill, requirement
quandary	difficulty, impasse
radiant	bright, glowing
rampant	rife, raging, unchecked
ratification	assent, acceptance, approval
rationale	reason, thinking, theory
reciprocate	return, share
recommendation	approval, praise
reconnaissance	survey, scrutiny
recuperate	recover, get well, rally
reduction	cut
redundant	extra, not needed
with regard to	on, about, as to
regimen	rule, system; diet
regret	be sorry

Plain Words

regulation	rule, law, bylaw
rehabilitate	redeem, straighten out, restore
reimburse	pay back, refund
reinforce	strengthen, brace, prop up
reiterate	repeat, say again
remainder	rest, others
remark	say
renegade	outlaw, crook, criminal
replica	copy, model
representative	agent, deputy
reprimand	rebuke, scold
repudiate	disown, reject, deny
require	need, call for, ask for
rescind	set aside, repeal, cancel
resemblance	likeness
reside	live, occupy, room
residence	house, home, apartment
respond	answer, reply
restrain	check, stop
retain	keep
retrench	cut down, reduce
retrieve	bring back, recover
reveal	show
rupture	break, snap
sanguine	optimistic, confident
sanitary	healthful, clean, germ-free
saturate	soak, fill, drench
segment	part
selection	choice, pick
self-confessed	confessed
significant	serious, grave
similar	like
situated	placed, put, housed
socialize	mingle, meet, make friends
solicit	ask for, beg, canvass
spacious	vast, roomy
spontaneous	unplanned, off the cuff, impulsive

Plain Words

state	say
stigma	stain, taint, disgrace
stimulate	arouse, stir up, excite
stringent	strict, tight
submit	give, send
subordinate	helper, assistant
subsequently	later, after that
substantiate	prove, support, back up
sufficient	enough, plenty, ample
suffocate	smother, choke
summon	send for
superficial	shallow, slight, flimsy
supersede	replace, displace
in short supply	scarce
supportive of	support
sustain	suffer, bear
syndrome	symptoms, clue
systematic	orderly, regular
technicality	detail, minor point
temperamental	moody, fickle, high-strung
terminal	fatal
terminate	end, stop
therapeutic	healing
toxic	poisonous, deadly
transform	change, alter
transmit	send
transparent	clear, lucid
traumatic	shocking
turbulent	stormy, wild, violent
ulterior	hidden
ultimate	last, final
underprivileged	poor, hard up
unfavourable	harmful, damaging, unpromising
unmistakable	clear, plain, evident
unpretentious	modest, humble
unveil	announce
updated	current
upgrade	improve, better

Plain Words

urbane	polished, well-bred, elegant
utilize	use
vacillate	waver, falter, hesitate
validity	truth, proof
vaunted	celebrated, famous
vehicle	car, truck, bus
velocity	speed
venue	place, site
verbatim	word for word, exactly
viable	workable, practical, usable
vicinity	near, close
visualize	see, foresee, imagine, picture
vulnerable	defenceless
withhold	hold back, refuse
withstand	bear, endure, resist, cope

Also available from The Canadian Press

The Canadian Press Stylebook
The CP Stylebook is the bible consulted by journalists at Canada's national news agency as they provide thousands of words of copy each day to newspapers, television stations, radio broadcasters and Internet sites. It is also an indispensable guide for public relations writers, corporate communicators, civil servants, magazine editors and students - in fact, just about anyone looking for practical answers to questions on writing and editing. Paperback, 448 pages.

CP Caps and Spelling on CD-ROM
The contents of Caps and Spelling in a searchable onscreen format. Works with both Windows and Mac.

Guide du journaliste
For journalists and others working in French. This is not a translation of the CP Stylebook, but written in French, focused on French style and writing issues. Paperback, 200 pages.

BN Style Guide
If you want to learn to write for the ear, then this is book to consult. Since 1978, the Broadcast News Style Guide has been the reference for anyone working in broadcasting or wishing to work in broadcasting. Paperback, 265 pages.

For further information:
Internet: www.cp.org
Phone orders: 1-800-434-7578
E-mail: books@cp.org